History of France

An Enthralling Overview of Major Events and Figures

Free limited time bonus

Stop for a moment. We have a free bonus set up for you. The problem is this: we forget 90% of everything that we read after 7 days. Crazy fact, right? Here's the solution: we've created a printable, 1-page pdf summary for this book that you're reading now. All you have to do to get your free pdf summary is to go to the following website:

https://livetolearn.lpages.co/enthrallinghistory/

Once you do, it will be intuitive. Enjoy, and thank you!

Table of Contents

Introduction: France – A Rich Tapestry of History

France has always been a melting pot mixture of people, and its early history included the Celts and Greeks. In fact, the Greeks, fresh from the Mediterranean, founded the city of Marseille in 600 BCE in the reaches of southern France. In the meantime, the Celts began to pour in from the north and would take over much of the rest of what we now know as France, even while the shores of southern France would remain a Mediterranean hub of Romans and Greeks.

The advance of the Celts would only be checked when Julius Caesar took on the dreaded Gaul leader Vercingetorix, coming out on top in 52 BCE. After the province of Roman Gaul was established, many Roman-styled cities were founded, such as Lyon, which would be outfitted with the latest Greco-Roman stylings of theaters, circuses, and public bathhouses.

The locals readily mingled, mixing Celtic and Roman cultures and genealogies. Latin became the dominate language in the meantime, overwriting the more traditional dialects of the region. It was from these Latin roots that the language of French would eventually develop. But as the Roman Empire declined and barbarian Franks and Visigoths besieged Roman Gaul on all sides, Gaul became destined to transform into France, and needless to say, France would go through some rather significant changes along the way.

Today, France benefits from this patchwork, from the Celts of Gaul to Imperial Rome to the Franks to its successive line of kings to the French Revolution and beyond—all of these created the French identity. Even though some of these threads seem as if they are at odds with each other, such as the French kings of old and the revolution that toppled them, both are celebrated for what they had to offer the rich tapestry of France.

For this reason, visitors to France today might just be treated to a commemoration of King Louis XIV (AKA the Sun King), only to witness a raucous celebration of "Bastille Day," which saw the royal monarchy's overthrow. Suffice it to say, France is complex, and its history reflects that fact. In the following chapters, we will unravel all of these unique threads of the French experience and identity as we examine them one by one.

Chapter 1: From Prehistory to the Roman Empire

Even though we do not have a written record from the earliest period of human habitation in France, there are indeed plenty of indications of France's lively, prehistoric past. The rock walls of French caves bear stunning testament to that. For just a brief look into the walled caverns of a site such as the "Lascaux Caves" with its stunning imagery of bulls running across open fields, and one knows that even tens of thousands of years ago, clever, imaginative people called this part of the world home.

It was here that their hopes and dreams were kindled, and their minds sought to explore their surroundings. The paintings found at "Lascaux" are so stunning that some have dubbed it the "Sistine Chapel of Prehistory." Even back in prehistory, before writing was invented, human beings were still just as desperate to tell a good story. And the rock walls of plenty of caves in France were the medium through which these narratives were so painstakingly relayed.

The message that the paintings in Lascaux seem to convey is one of freedom, majesty, and power. This can be felt through the remarkable vistas of powerful horses and bison charging across the terrain. It is believed that the prehistoric French of this period likely subsisted on fish more than anything else, yet in their art, fish was not the focus. The main focus was the animals that were largely unobtainable to them. They likely stared in wonder as these big beasts charged across fields in the distance.

These dynamic animals captured their attention the most, and it was their free and unbridled energy that they wished to leave a permanent testament of their free spirit was an aspiration of their own. Just imagine ancient man hunkered down in a cave, hiding from the elements and potential predators, dreaming of one day being able to charge out onto the open plains of France just like those wild beasts free to run.

One day, ancient man would leave the caves behind entirely and embark upon civilization. Human cities would dot the landscape, and the environment would be mostly bent to the will of humanity.

The Celts were the first known people to make a significant effort at taming the wilderness of prehistoric France. It is said that the Celts, who likely originated from farther inland in Central Europe, arrived in the Paris region and began to use the Seine River near the site of the modern-day French capital.

The Romans who encountered these migrants would refer to them as "Gauli" or "Gauls," Roman words that meant *barbarian*. As such things might imply, the Romans did not look too highly at the Celts of France, and as much as they tried to lump them all together, the Gauls were not a unified force.

The Gauls made up several tribes that often fought against each other, and the Romans often attempted to exploit this fact to their full advantage. Julius Caesar would be the most successful at this, noting that there were three main divisions of Gauls, and he would often play one of these divisions off on the other. Caesar insisted that his eventual invasion of Gaul was primarily a *preemptive* exercise.

He is said to have done this because the Gauls of France often launched raids into northern Italy. When Caesar launched his massive attack on Gaul in 58 BCE, he insisted that it was only to stop the Gauls from launching further raids on Roman territory. As much as some historians may want to write all of this off as political rhetoric on Caesar's part, there is some truth to these assertions. The Roman peace, after all, was only achieved through absolute control of surrounding territories.

The only way Rome could ensure its citizens' safety from Gallic raids was to place Gaul under Rome's control. Much the same thing could be said for the regions of North Africa that Rome later conquered. Until mighty Carthage and other powerful neighbors were subdued, there was always the threat of war. Even worse, the irregular warfare of pirates and raiders could sneak into the Mediterranean and affect Roman citizens as well.

For the Romans, the only way to ensure peace was to dominate and control all of their regional neighbors, and as Roman soldiers marched all around the Mediterranean, eventually turning it into a Roman lake, that is precisely what they did! The invasion and conquest of French Gaul can be said to be one of the first major steps in this process.

There were, of course, great ulterior motives in taking Gaul and establishing Roman garrisons to ensure that there would be no further incursions into Roman lands. Gaul was rich in resources, which would help fuel the expansion of first the Roman Republic and, ultimately, the Roman Empire.

The war against the Gauls also famously benefited Julius Caesar himself. His victories gave him valuable military experience that would serve him well when he later fought to become the supreme leader of the Roman Republic. Every time he returned to Rome in an elaborate triumph (fresh from his latest victories on the western frontier), he was likely preparing himself for the most significant conquest of all: Rome itself.

Fighting in Gaul gave him both political clout and an army that would loyally serve his own interests when it came to that. The clash between the Romans and the Gauls amounted to a titanic clash of civilizations. The Romans had more advanced infrastructure and weaponry, but the Gauls had the numbers and the sheer ferocity (not to mention superb horsemanship) to give the legions of Rome a huge challenge.

Subduing the Gauls would not have been an easy task for anyone, but Julius Caesar was willing to take up the challenge. In these efforts, the main antagonist to rise up against Caesar was the Gaul chieftain: Vercingetorix.

During one of Caesar's first face-offs with Vercingetorix, he lost whole legions of Roman troops to the Gauls. The Gaul leader was not only a fierce fighter and director of fellow warriors but also a long-term strategist who could anticipate the big picture involved in the uphill struggle that the Gauls faced. Vercingetorix knew that the Gauls faced a fighting force with significant advantages; he knew that the Gauls had to maximize any advantages they could claim.

One of the Gauls' primary advantages was that they were fighting on their own home turf. They knew the terrain, and they knew how to best make use of it. Experts at the ambush, they could swoop down on their steeds and catch the Romans entirely off-guard. Vercingetorix was also sure to take advantage of the terrain even when he and his troops faced defeat.

For example, if they were forced to give ground, the departing Gauls were sure to destroy whatever territory they had to give up. They deployed a systematic "scorched earth" policy, which had them setting whole fields ablaze just so the Romans would not be able to benefit from the grain grown there. Vercingetorix only failed in these efforts when he was overruled by several chieftains over the burning of a wealthy Gallic province called Avaricum.

Vercingetorix did not want all this wealth to fall into Caesar's hands, but his fellow commanders could not stomach the thought of destroying it. When the Gauls were forced to depart, the Romans received this unexpected boon to exploit to their full advantage. Ultimately, Caesar was successful, and Vercingetorix was defeated and paraded around during Caesar's subsequent triumph in Rome.

In 52 BCE, the Gauls of France were all but conquered by the Romans. This conquest was not as crushing as one might expect since the Romans were rather inclusive; they were not typically in the business of displacing people but rather doing all they could to *incorporate conquered peoples* into the Roman Empire. And for Gauls, who played the game of the Romans and jumped through all of the hoops that had been set before them, there were indeed advantages in becoming Roman citizens.

By the 1st century, Roman civilization was firmly a part of life in Gaul. No sooner than the Roman way of life was entrenched, it began to be slowly overlaid with something more significant (some would say *much more significant*). In that very century, an itinerant preacher from Galilee, known as Jesus Christ, would usher in a new religion that would take the Roman world by storm.

Jesus lived, died, and, as Christians would tell it, was *resurrected* during the first half of the 1st century. The religion of Christianity was founded and began to flourish in the Mideast shortly after that. It took some time for Christian evangelists to spread this new religion, but thanks to the safety and security of Roman roads, the Gospel ultimately reached all parts of the Roman Empire. And by the dawning of the 2nd century, the people of Gaul were quite familiar with it.

Upon being converted to Christianity, the Gauls could be quite formidable fighters for the faith, as demonstrated by the Bishop of Paris, Saint Denis, who was martyred around the year 250. Denis and his colleagues are said to have been so effective in preaching the gospel that their frustrated pagan competitors complained to the Roman governor and insisted that he do something about it.

The fact that Saint Denis' martyrdom only came after he was tattled on by local rivals is consistent with how Christian persecution typically occurred in the pre-Christian Roman Empire. Besides specific programs of persecution issued by the likes of Nero and Diocletian, for the most part, most Roman officials operated under a hands-off policy when it came to the Christians.

It was advised to forego seeking them out; instead, it was best to ignore Christians unless specific issues were brought to their attention. As such, it was typically only when neighbors (or, as in Saint Denis case, pagan competitors) called Christians to their attention, that action was taken. The Roman governor likely would have been blissfully ignorant of Saint Denis and his Christian followers unless the locals had not complained about him.

They railed against the Christians as a threat to Gaul's status quo, so the Roman Governor was reluctantly pressured to take action. Even then, a Christian still had plenty of chances to get off the hook. As was famously demonstrated in the account of the martyrdom of Polycarp. During Polycarp's martyrdom, the elder Polycarp was practically begged by the Roman officials to simply proclaim Caesar was God and be done with it, so they could let him go.

The officials did not care so much if Polycarp continued to secretly carry on as a Christian as long as he made a public declaration in solidarity with the emperor so they could send a report back to Rome that they had restored order. Polycarp, of course, was not willing to do any such thing, so he was executed. Much the same could be said for the martyrdom of Saint Denis.

Like Polycarp, Saint Denis refused to retract his faith, and after two years of imprisonment, he was executed. He was led outside of his cell and positioned on a high hill, where a Roman soldier had him kneel before being decapitated. But according to popular legend, this wasn't the end of the story. It is said that the martyred saint picked up the head, stood, and began preaching the gospel again!

It might be a bit hard for us to believe such things today, but nevertheless, the martyrdom of Saint Denis stood out, and the same hill where he met his fate was named after him, referred to in France as "Montmartre." This name is believed to be derived from the Latin words "Mons Martyrum" which translates as "Martyrs' Mountain."

The Christians of Gaul would not have to wait long for their deliverance. In 313, due to a special edict made in Milan by joint emperors Constantine and Licinius, it was deemed that the Christian religion would receive official tolerance throughout the Empire. This meant that the Christians of Gaul no longer had to fear getting on the wrong side of their pagan neighbors.

Yes, now Christian Gauls could accidentally prune their pagan neighbor's tree in peace without fear of the grumpy neighbors reporting them to Roman authorities out of sheer spite. Now they could breathe. And after Constantine became the sole authority of the Roman Empire, he saw to it that Christianity was not just tolerated but became the driving force of the empire itself.

In the meantime, Gallic France would become a magnificent hub of culture and Christianity. Even so, the Roman Empire was well past its prime, and by the dawning of the 5th century, the frontier regions were under constant assault by various warring tribes. The primary antagonists were the Germanic tribal groups of the Ostrogoths, Visigoths, and Vandals.

Of these, the Vandals stand out the most to the modern eye since the words "vandal" and "vandalize" used in common parlance today derive from the Vandals themselves. The Vandals were quite good at conducting sudden raids, and ambushes, in which they smashed windows, burned buildings, and generally destroyed everything in their path. In other words, they totally *vandalized* the place!

But even so, the Vandals actually became the friendliest of these invaders to Rome. Most of the Vandals had become Christians by this time, although their brand of Christianity differed from the Catholic faith espoused by Rome. The Vandals had come into contact with a different variation of the belief system rejected by the Catholics; they followed the teachings of Arius.

Arius believed that Jesus was not equal and one with God through the Trinity, contrary to what Catholics believe. Instead, Arius insisted that Jesus was created by Father God and therefore was secondary to him.

Those who followed this faith variant were called Arians and technically considered heretics by the Roman Catholic Church.

So even though the Vandals had some things in common with Rome, the differences they harbored were still more than capable of driving a wedge between the two civilizations. Even so, the Vandals were looked upon more favorably than a group like the Huns, who hailed from Mongolia, whose customs and way of life appeared much more alien to the Romans than the Vandals.

It was Atilla the Hun whose armies would pose a dire threat to the Romans in the 450s. Atilla and his horde would ultimately be put down, primarily thanks to Roman auxiliary units composed of Vandals. It was after the Huns were put down, however, that the Vandals and other tribes would begin to take the Roman Empire over outright.

It was in 476 CE that the last Roman emperor, Romulus Augustus, was forced to step down. Although this is often referred to as the fall of the Roman Empire, only the Western Roman Empire fell. The Eastern, Greek-speaking half of the empire would live on. Even though Rome had fallen, the people of the Eastern Roman Empire considered themselves still part of *the* Roman Empire. Eventually, this half of the empire became known as the Byzantine Empire to help distinguish it from the Western Roman Empire.

However, there would be no return to the Roman fold as it pertains to Gaul.

Chapter 2: After the Fall of Rome

The Gauls were on their own after the fall of the Roman Empire. And in the power vacuum, various warlords, chieftains, and rulers would rise to prominence in various enclaves of Gaul. An early example of this leadership is the Frankish King Clovis. Becoming king of the Franks in 481, Clovis is often dubbed as France's very first true king

Clovis was a force to be reckoned with, seeing that he united almost all of what today constitutes modern-day France under his rule. At the time of his death in 513, it is said that much of the boundaries we know of as France, with the addition of modern-day Belgium, were under Clovis' thumb. Although Clovis is often seen as part of the process of toppling Roman rule, he was also a continuation of it in many ways.

He and his father, Childeric, had deep ties to the Roman military and political machine. In fact, Childeric was one of the leading generals of the Roman/Germanic army that successfully put down the threat of Atilla the Hun. Clovis likely would have continued joint participation with the Romans if it was not abundantly clear that the Roman Empire was in shambles.

Instead of holding up a falling house, Clovis decided to participate in its demolition. In this capacity, he took on a remnant of Roman and Gallic forces in 486, soundly defeating them at the Battle of Soissons. But they were not the only ones he defeated; he also crushed an army of Visigoths at Vouille around 507. A few years later, in 511, he had a city called Paris reconfigured to become the capital of his realm.

Clovis maintained much of the local Roman administration and customs throughout all of this. Although Clovis had defeated Roman soldiers in battle, he still understood the inherent value of Roman civil infrastructure and wished to keep much of it intact. Like many after him, Clovis considered himself not so much a usurper but somehow a continuation of the mighty Rome that he had toppled. Along with keeping Roman customs and civil bureaucracy, King Clovis also adopted the Roman Catholic faith of Christianity. It was in 496 that Clovis supposedly had a dramatic conversion to the faith. He was locked in battle against a barbarian army when it seemed his forces were about to come out on the losing end. In his desperation, he cried out to the Christian God of his wife, "Clotilda."

King Clovis' wife was already a Roman Catholic and had apparently been pestering Clovis to convert. According to Clovis, in the middle of this battle, he earnestly tried his wife's faith; it is said that he cried out to God, and suddenly the battle turned in his favor. He and his troops were victorious!

His conversion was a big deal since, as king, he had his subjects convert as well. This ensured that France, no matter the fate of the Roman Empire, would remain Roman Catholic. Clovis established a long line of rule in what has been dubbed the reign of the "Merovingian" kings. It is said that there were 27 of these so-called Merovingians leading all the way up to Childeric III, the last of the Merovingian line.

Childeric III was superseded by Pepin the Short, which marked the Carolingians' start. The Carolingians would rise to fame with the epic Carolingian monarch, Charlemagne the Great. A few names stand out between these dynastic lines, such as Dagobert I and Charles Martel. These leaders were known for either seizing land in new conquest or for their formidable defense and consolidation of what they already controlled.

Dagobert I is known for seizing Alsace, Vosges, and the Ardennes. The mighty Charles Martel was known for his staunch defense of the realm, especially after the rise of Islam when Martel prevented an invasion of Islamic armies. Even though Spain was overrun and captured, initiating a centuries-long Reconquista to take it back, France under Martel would be the speed bump that would slow down and ultimately stop the Islamic advance.

But who was Charles Martel? He was the illegitimate son of Pepin II, who, although not king in his own right, was a powerful count in the Merovingian kingdom, ruling his own corner of France. He was instrumental in saving the kingdom in 687 and restoring Merovingian rule that had been temporarily disrupted. Pepin II perished in 714, and when France was later beset with strife, it was to his son, Charles Martel, that France looked for its security.

Martel was a skilled and able military commander. First, he took on invading Germanic tribes in the north before sending his troops south to stop Islamic incursions that had spilled out of neighboring Spain. He was instrumental in halting the invaders at Poitiers in the year 732. Although this event occurred a few centuries before the start of the Crusades, the high praise and esteem Martel was given not just in France but all throughout the Christian world was similar to how the Crusaders would be viewed.

Martel was viewed as not just a skilled warrior who had halted an invasion but as nothing short of a champion of God who had prevented the destruction of Christianity itself. It was quite clear that the brilliant Carolingian dynasty of Charles Martel was destined to outshine the Merovingian dynasty, whose fading sun had already begun to set. But the Carolingians were not going to topple their predecessors, as was done with the Romans.

On the contrary, the Carolingians initially tried to prop the failing Merovingians up and only superseded them when there was not much of any other choice. After Martel's death in 737, his sons Carloman and Pepin III worked hard to suppress revolts in the kingdom and take on outside threats, even while propping up the final Merovingian king, Childeric III. For the time being, they were quite content to wield their military might behind the façade of Childeric III.

It was only in 747, when this situation was no longer tenable, that Pepin III (otherwise known as Pepin the Short) became the first Carolingian king of France. His brother Carloman returned to an abbey in Monte Cassino, Italy, ceding all power to his little but mighty brother, Pepin the Short. Pepin was a grand strategist who set the stage for what would come.

Pepin was the first to establish the practice of creating an assembly of nobles to actually "vote" for him to become king. He was also the first to seek out and receive the official backing of the pope. Pepin, in return, repaid the pope's kindness by granting him land in Central Italy that had just been taken from Pepin's enemies; this land would ultimately become the Papal States.

Pope Stephen II officially gave his blessing to the Carolingian crown in 751. Some historians have noted that this is also quite important for the later French kings since this was when the notion of absolutist rule by "divine right" was first developed. After Pepin's demise in 768, his son, the great Charlemagne, became his successor.

Charlemagne would continue the legacy of combining martial and military might with the strength of a unified Catholic faith. In many ways, Charlemagne would kickstart precursors to both the Crusades and the Inquisition in the way he handled the pagan, Germanic tribes in his northern frontiers. For it was Charlemagne that ruthlessly charged into Saxony and took on the pagan Norse, not only waging war against their armies but against their religion itself.

During this conflict, he ordered the destruction of pagan shrines, most infamously, the Irminsul in modern-day Denmark. According to the Norse religion, the Irminsul was a sacred tree or pillar representing the tree of life. It was said among the Norse that if Irminsul ever fell, Ragnarök (the Norse version of Armageddon) would begin.

So, when Charlemagne had this thing burned down to the ground, it probably is not a coincidence that the Viking raids out of Scandinavia that would shake Europe to its core began shortly thereafter. The Vikings apparently felt that they were waging a holy war of their own against the Christian King Charlemagne, and the destruction of Irminsul likely had a hand in triggering it.

At any rate, Charlemagne ultimately succeeded in overrunning Saxony, and that was when his version of the Inquisition began. It was not enough for him to have his conquered subjects pay lip service to Christianity; they had to prove their faith. And if inquiries were made, and one was not deemed to be Christian enough, Charlemagne was not above having them executed.

As mentioned, it could be argued that such things set part of the precedent and the groundwork for both the later Crusades and the Inquisition. At any rate, Charlemagne's greatest boon as it pertained to shaping the dynamic between church and state came in the year 800, when Pope Leo III, beset with his own problems, decided to crown Charlemagne as emperor.

Pope Leo III certainly appreciated Charlemagne's efforts of both spreading and protecting the Christian faith, and he was in dire need of Charlemagne's protection. Pope Leo III was nearly killed by an angry mob just before he crowned Charlemagne. Ever since the fall of the Roman Empire, the Roman Catholic Church had been in a precarious position.

No longer ensured protection by Romans, the pope had to often play local power players against each other in a never-ending Machiavellian bid to stay afloat. However, not all of the popes were always successful in these machinations, and after Pope Leo III ran afoul of a sect of cardinals who had the backing of an aggressive warlord, Pope Leo himself was in danger. He was traveling down the streets of Rome when he was nearly assaulted.

The only thing that saved him was that some of Charlemagne's troops happened to be present, coming to the rescue at the last minute in what must have seemed like a miracle. Pope Leo III cannily realizing who had his back, decided to throw in his lot with Charlemagne entirely, declaring him emperor. No Western ruler had been declared as such since the fall of the western half of the Roman Empire.

In the meantime, the Byzantine successors of the Eastern Roman Empire were quite incensed and criticized Leo to no end. But any threats from the Byzantines at this point were empty and worthless. The Byzantines in faraway Greece were not in any position to defend the pope, let alone attack him. So, Pope Leo III threw in his lot with Charlemagne. This would be the start of what would ultimately become known as the *Holy Roman Empire.*

It is surprising how little many know about the Holy Roman Empire, but this conglomerate of Western and Central European states would become a significant player in world affairs until its ultimate dissolution in the early 1800s. At any rate, this was a big deal, and besides realigning papal authority with Western power, the shockwaves of Pope Leo's backing of Charlemagne also put the first cracks in the façade that Western and Eastern Christianity were united in a universal "Catholic" faith.

The Eastern Christians would begin to view themselves as orthodox originalists and the Catholics as usurpers; the strain that started with the crowning of Charlemagne would continue until the official schism of 1054 separated the Eastern and Western churches for good. At any rate,

Charlemagne was a force to be reckoned with. By his passing in 814, he had managed to subdue roughly all of modern-day France and what now constitutes Germany and much of northern Italy.

Charlemagne controlled the largest territory in Western Europe since the days of the Western Roman Empire, so to call him an emperor was no stretch of the imagination. The biggest issue after his passing was how to hold onto and consolidate all of Charlemagne's gains. Fortunately for his successors, Charlemagne had laid out much of the groundwork himself.

Before his demise, Charlemagne took an active role in administration. He traveled widely to install and instruct local administrators and, perhaps more importantly, created a council of nobility that would regularly meet to discuss how best to administer their sections of the empire. Charlemagne is also credited with boosting the intelligentsia of his realm by funding the building of monasteries and encouraging them to become workshops of literacy, in which ancient manuscripts were transcribed and new ones were composed.

It is said that during this period, Charlemagne's monks developed the system of upper- and lower-case letters for the Latin alphabet, as we know them today. It was with the official script's retooling that the region's spoken dialect began to be refined as well. Around this time, the so-called "Old French" first came into vogue. For all of his significant gains, at Charlemagne's death in 814, the economy faced a downturn, and the large amount of land inherited by his successor, Louis the Pious, proved far too unwieldy for him to control on his own.

As such, in 817, he determined to divide his spoils among his three sons. Louis meant for the land to be divvied up after his death, but the fighting over the territory began while he was still alive! In this dynastic struggle, the sons turned against their father and ultimately turned against each other as they battled it out for supremacy. The strife only ended with the Treaty of Verdun in the year 843.

This treaty officially divided the empire between the three heirs of Louis. Louis' son "Charles the Bald" received the territory then known as "West Francia," which constituted much of what we now refer to as modern-day "France." In the meantime, Charles the Bald's brother Louis was given control of "East Francia," which consisted of much of what would later become modern-day Germany.

Lothair (the other brother) was ceded what was then called Lotharingia, a narrow but long stretch of territory that ran directly between West and East Francia. Lotharingia is perhaps the most fascinating kingdom that came into being since it ran from Belgium and the Netherlands to its northernmost extent; then, as it advanced south, it cut through parts of eastern France and western Germany, as it stretched on past the Alps and into northern Italy. All these things set the stage for the new kingdom of France that was about to form.

Chapter 3: A New Kingdom

It was no sooner than the dust had settled over the Treaty of Verdun in 843 that the successor state of the former Carolingian empire—West Francia—was subjected to several incursions by outside antagonists. Throughout much of the 9th and 10th centuries, the region would face several invasions from far and wide. Islamic armies, Viking raiders, and Hungarian warriors would all test their metal against the blades of the French.

But out of all these threats, it was always the Vikings (or, as they were often referred to the "Northmen" or "Norsemen") who would pose the greatest threat. Ever since Charlemagne stirred up the hornet's nest of the Norse people in the upper reaches of Scandinavia, swarms of Vikings had descended from the North. And whether it was all part of an intentional plan or just happenstance, the descendants of the same Norse people that Charlemagne had insulted would indeed reach the former heart of his empire in West Francia.

All throughout the 840s, the Norse would wreak havoc, raiding French cities, and in 851, they would sack Paris. The Norse would then make permanent encampments along the lower Seine; this would lead to Charles the Simple, who pragmatically realized the difficulty of his own situation, negotiating a truce with the Viking leader Rollo by granting his Norse warriors a long strip of France's western coast, which after that would be dubbed *Normandy*.

The name is derived from the Latin *Northmanni*, which translates into English as simply "Northmen." As much of a blow as this might have been to French esteem, Charles the Simple's gamble paid off, and the Norse proved fairly good neighbors. Rollo was made a duke and became a Christian who swore allegiance to the king of France.

Even so, the Carolingian dynasty had already been disrupted. The end came not through war but through a simple vote by an assembly of notables in 888 which had chosen Robert the Strong as their king. This Robertian dynastic line would lead Hugh Capet to become king of France in 987. But although he is now known as a king of France, at the time, he was more likely to call himself "King of the Franks."

What is the difference, one might ask? Although surrounding regions were arguably his vassals, the only land that Hugh Capet directly controlled was a swath of territory surrounding Paris. And the outlying regions were so hostile and unpredictable that it has been said that his venturing into them would have been fraught with difficulty. Things were so bad that some have likened his condition to almost akin to being under house arrest!

French historian and writer John Julius said:

> *"Between Paris and Orleans, he possessed towns and estates extending over four hundred square miles; there were also a couple of small properties near Angers and Chartres. But nowhere else in France was it safe for him to travel; to do so would have been to risk almost certain capture, and though his life might perhaps have been spared he was sure to be held to ransom - quite probably in extremely unpleasant conditions. 'Charlemagne's successor,' remarked a contemporary, 'did not dare leave home.' It was doubtless this uncertainty, this constant feeling of living a lie, that prevented him from ever calling himself King of France; nor indeed did any of his successor do so until Philip Augustus at the end of the twelfth century. 'King of the Franks' - Roi des Francs - was the title with which he was crowned; and King of the Franks he remained."*

Interestingly enough, if this first of the line of Capet was essentially a hostage under house arrest, it is indeed then quite ironic that the last of the Capets, King Louis XVI, who was killed during the French Revolution, also ended his days under house arrest! Toward the end, King Louis XVI tried to leave his palace on a couple of occasions only to be thwarted and turned back. It could therefore be said that it was not safe for a Capet then, nor for a Capet under Hugh Capet's rule either!

Although his kingdom had shrunk considerably, it was Hugh Capet, who was actually a great-grandson of Robert the Strong, who would start the "Capetian Dynasty" that would last all the way until King Louis XVI and Marie Antoinette lost their heads in the French Revolution of the 1790s. Considering how long this dynastic line lasted, it seems that Charles the Simple was not so simple after all, as his gambit actually paid off.

For the Norman invaders, instead of toppling France, they were ultimately absorbed into the larger patchwork of French society. Even so, it would take some time for this absorption to be complete, and in the early phases, there was undoubtedly much potential for the duke of Normandy to go rogue. This most famously occurred in 1066, when the Norman invasion of England was launched.

In the words of W. Scott Haine, a well-known researcher and writer on French history, the king of France "was little more than a spectator" as this spectacular conquest was undertaken by one of his vassals. As has often been somewhat cynically stated, the Middle Ages of Europe could be summed up as "Vassals and Castles." That is to say, it was from this point forward that feudalism reigned supreme.

France's duke of Normandy may have been an outlier in the independence and strength it demonstrated, but in truth, all of France was a patchwork of feudal landlords who, although swearing their allegiance to the king of France, were indeed in direct control of the land they occupied and administered it and the people that lived therein as they saw fit. It was not always the most pleasant of arrangements, and the welfare of citizens entirely hinged on the kindness (or unkindness) of those lording over them.

But the alternative was not any better for the average person of the time. Without the might of a local lord and his armies in place to protect his subject's life and whatever meager possessions they might have had, they would have been entirely on their own. And in these dark and hard times, peasants simply existing of their own accord in some field somewhere would be open to repeated attacks and raids by any armed bandits that just so happened to be passing through.

As such, most accepted the fate of being a vassal to a strong feudal landlord in return for the protection that the strong walls of their castle and the swords of their knights might provide. As simple as it was, this was the basic social compact of the day. However, the periodic warfare between local lords often became too much for the more peaceful-minded to countenance.

Such things led the church to actually step in, in 989 when church councils initiated the so-called "Peace of God" movement in an attempt to bring about the possibility of non-violent mediation to conflict. This movement was revived in 1027 with the "Truce of God" movement. This movement also took the step to declare that there should be no fighting on holy days such as Lent, Advent, Easter, and Sundays.

As well-intentioned as this was, the fact that folks wanted to kill each other (but only put it off because it was Sunday) likely made the cynical even more cynical. The only thing that slowed feudal warfare down was when in the year 1095, a certain French pope named Urban II called for a Crusade against the forces of Islam. Again, the cynical might point out that perhaps the best solution to stop all this infighting of Christians against Christians was to unite them against a common foe.

But as cynical as we might want to be, and Pope Urban II likely did consider such a thing, we cannot forget that the Crusades were much more complicated than that. As convenient as the Crusades might have been for this particular problem, the pope did not randomly attack Islamic forces only to unite feudal Christendom. The pope was answering a call for help from the Christian Byzantines of Constantinople (later conquered and renamed Istanbul), who were being overrun and attacked by Muslim armies.

The call for a Crusade was initially provoked by Muslim aggression against Constantinople, but the pope then sweetened the deal by declaring that the Holy Land of the Levant, which had fallen to Muslim forces in the 7th century, should also be reclaimed. The fact that the Crusades united the previously fickle and fractious feudal Christians can be considered an added benefit of this call to action but not the actual reason behind it.

Nevertheless, the French (or, as they were still often called, the Franks) bore the brunt of this enterprise. The vast bulk of the Crusaders sent were indeed French, and this was particularly true during the First Crusade. The subsequent crusades would then have their numbers bolstered by English and German Crusaders, but the French would always provide a large contingent of manpower. And when the Crusaders managed to rip Jerusalem (along with several other cities) from the Muslims' grasp, they made a French noble, Godfrey of Bouillon, the king of the newly established "Kingdom of Jerusalem."

The fact that the victors of this conflict immediately fell back on the feudal patterns they were used to is a testament to how fundamentally ingrained this form of governance was. They realized that the faraway king of France would not be able to administer Jerusalem, so immediately, they set out to establish their own local potentate to administer the newly conquered realm. Godfrey was not interested in being called "king" since he felt he was unworthy of such a thing.

As such, he was officially referred to as "Defender of the Holy Sepulcher" instead. Even though unofficially, behind the scenes, he was indeed referred to as the king of Jerusalem, whether he liked it or not. The man they chose for this role was only destined to live on for another year before he abruptly perished, instigating a minor crisis, until the nobles found someone else to take up the challenge.

Regarding the Crusades, the Mideast was not the *only* region in which the French launched them. In the early 1200s, when widespread heresy erupted in the southwestern corner of France known as the "Languedoc," French troops were sent in. The *Albigensian Crusade* had begun at the behest of the pope.

This Crusade was waged against a religious sect known as the Cathars, who were essentially a modified version of Christian Gnosticism, which subscribed to the notion of pantheism. Pantheism is the belief that virtually everyone and everything is a manifestation of God. Although many Christians would subscribe to the concept that Jesus Christ was a manifestation of God, the idea that *we all are* a part of that same manifestation would strike most as absurd and indeed heretical.

But this is precisely what the Cathars believed. Even worse, as far as the Catholic Church was concerned, was the Cathar belief in *dualism,* which spoke of the goodness of God being equal to the evilness of Satan. This seemed to be a rather alarming equivocation for Catholics; to them, it was as if the Cathars were preaching that the devil was an equal to the Almighty. It is understandable why the Catholic Church might call such a belief out.

At any rate, the main focal point of this Crusade, which began in earnest in 1208, was in and around the city of Toulouse. It was here that the Cathar variant of Gnosticism absolutely thrived. The pope was serious about stamping out this strain, so much so that he sent his own papal legate, Arnaud Amalric, to oversee the operation. In the correspondence between him and the pope, Amalric gleefully reported the Cathars' destruction and thanked him for eliminating what he termed "pestilential enemies."

Indeed, the Cathars of France were viewed as a deadly plague that needed to be wiped out before their supposedly "heretical beliefs" spread any further. This was considered important enough that a vast contingent of France's best knights was used to crush the Albigensian sect once and for all. The Albigensian Crusade only ended in 1229 through the signing of the Treaty of Paris.

The future French king's (Louis IX's) mom, Blanche of Castille, played a part in arranging the termination of this bloody affair. Twenty years after the Albigensian Crusade had concluded, her son Louis IX led the *Seventh Crusade* all the way to Egypt in 1248. This mission was led by French King Louis IX. Louis IX would later be known as Saint Louis, and there is a reason for this: he was extremely devout and pious—some might even say zealous—about the Christian faith.

Much of Louis IX's enthusiasm for the Crusades can be traced back to a sickness he had contracted. The illness apparently almost spelled the end for the king, and on his sickbed, he supposedly vowed to go on a Crusade if he recovered. He did indeed recover. And as a consequence, he considered the crusade the least he could do for his restored health.

This Seventh Crusade had an entirely different thrust than the First Crusade. Since the days of the First Crusade, the Holy Land had already been all but lost. Jerusalem was lost to the Crusaders in 1187, and by the 1240s, they had what really only amounted to a toe hold on the northwestern corner of the Levant. Considering that it was Jerusalem that the Crusaders so desperately wanted to take back, one might naturally wonder why the Crusaders did not head to Jerusalem outright.

But there was a reason for that: Louis IX was convinced that it would be easier to establish a base in Egypt, march up through the Sinai to Palestine, and then head for Jerusalem from the south. In 1249, the French king's forces landed in Egypt, and Egyptian forces met the French almost immediately. These forces were being directed by the Egyptian commander Fakhr al-Din. Initially, the French were good at overwhelming and pushing the Egyptian general's troops back. And interestingly enough, they were able to then take the Egyptian city of Damietta without a fight since Fakhr al-Din ordered it to be completely evacuated.

But as much as this might have seemed like a win for the French Crusaders, it was actually a part of the longer strategy of Fakhr al-Din. He knew full well that the French would have a tough time holding and maintaining the city, especially once the hot summer season had begun to take hold and resources would be scarce. So it was that the wily Egyptian general figured that he would move his troops further up north along the Nile River to a garrison called "al-Mansurah" to consolidate his strength and allow the Crusading invaders downwind to become weaker.

He was more than content to wait them out and let them perish, even while daring them to come out into the open and confront him and his troops in an open battle that they were sure to lose. In the meantime, the Egyptian sultan, al-Salih, had abruptly perished. This could have been a boon for French morale, but only if they had known that the event had occurred. But once again, bearing testament to just how wise a strategist Fakhr al-Din was, he kept all news of the sultan's passing absolutely quiet while he essentially served as the head of state.

Louis and his knights finally lost their patience waiting it out in Damietta, and on Christmas Day, they marched on up to engage their opponents at al-Mansurah. Both forces now faced each other from opposite banks of the river. They hurled arrows and stones at one another, even with water between them.

This standoff continued for some time, until the spring of 1250 when a narrow part of the river was discovered that could be successfully crossed on horseback. However, their crossing did not go unnoticed, and Louis and his men noticed a small contingent of Egyptian scouts watching them. The Crusaders took off in pursuit, even though not all of their troops had crossed.

Disastrously enough, they chased the small group of spies all the way to al-Mansurah itself. This played exactly into Fakhr al-Din's hands, as he could now battle the Crusaders on his own home turf. The Crusaders were ultimately decimated, and disorderly withdrawal began on April 5th. The Crusaders were seen running down the Nile River's banks as their enemy stabbed and shot arrows into their backs.

But the worst was yet to come, as King Louis IX was taken prisoner in the confusion. This led to a massive amount of money being demanded for the king's return. For this king's ransom, the French had to raid their own Templar Knights' coffers to get the funds to pay the ransom. Louis ultimately returned to France in 1254 a sad, broken, and disappointed man.

Still, he would try again in 1270. This time around, however, the older King Louis barely even made it to Egypt, and he perished shortly after he arrived due to illness. Ironically it was an illness that had him embark upon Egypt in the first place, and it was an illness that terminated his mission. Nevertheless, he was revered by the French for his dedication to the cause of Christianity and was later declared a saint.

For this reason, there are countless cities, such as "St. Louis, Missouri" or bodies of water, such as the "St. Louis River" that bear this French monarch's name. The great Saint Louis was succeeded by King Philip III. Most historians agree that not much of note occurred during his reign. During the much more eventful reign of Philip IV, a terrible conflict with the Catholic Church was launched in 1285.

Philip IV wished to gain the upper hand over the pope regarding who had the final say in matters of Court and country. Philip tried to resurrect Roman law that considered the "king's wish" as "the law's wish." But Pope Boniface VIII quickly pointed out that the pope was technically given authority by God "over all temporal rulers." This led to a strange and hostile struggle between the French church and state that did not exist before. And it only ended when Pope Boniface perished in 1303.

His successor Benedict XI would last roughly a year before he perished on July 7, 1304. He was succeeded by a pope who would be much more pliant to the French king's demands: Pope Clement V. It was in this backdrop of intrigue and uncertainty that the French state and the Roman Catholic Church would play a part in another infamous event: the dissolution of the Knights Templar. For it was in 1307 that this same power-hungry French King, Philip IV, bullied Pope Clement V to work in concert with him to condemn the Knights Templar for heresy.

The Knights leaders were arrested and under torture, forced to admit that they were heretics. The more cynical will note, however, that the king owed the knights quite a bit of money from previous crusading enterprises, and it could very well be that he just did not want to pay the Templars back!

The Templars were officially dissolved in 1312 at his and the pope's orders. Jacques de Molay, the 23rd and last Grandmaster of the Knights Templar, was executed in 1314.

The execution was a horrid affair in which the former Grandmaster of the Order was burned alive. Before he perished, he fully recanted any admission of guilt and instead placed responsibility firmly at the feet of King Philip and Pope Clement. As if he had been suddenly endowed with the gift of prophecy, the burning Grandmaster is said to have suddenly declared that both the king of France and the pope would die before the year was out.

He then laid out a general curse on France for several generations. Seeing that both King Philip and Pope Clement did indeed die in 1314, the words of the Grandmaster must have been quite chilling to contemplate in retrospect. And the situation for France did not improve with the deaths of these two men; in fact, it got much worse. There was an economic downturn between the years 1315 and 1317.

If Philip thought that looting the coffers of the Templars would help the French economy, he was proved dramatically wrong. The French had to resort to high taxation, which only made the situation worse. In this backdrop of uncertainty and discontent, the Hundred Years' War erupted in 1337. A few years later, France would be hit by the Black Plague, a scourge that would kill off a significant portion of the French population, further exacerbating economic problems due to a lack of skilled workers.

If the Grandmaster did indeed curse France as is claimed, such things are rather convincing of his words' effect. Adding to these problems, France faced a succession crisis after Philip the Fair's death in 1328. The crisis was not immediately apparent since Philip had three children to succeed him; the problem was that his offspring seemed unable to produce heirs of their own.

This resulted in all three children of Philip the Fair ruling consecutively until the last one perished. And shockingly enough, they each died one after the other in the same year! After the last of them died with no heir, the struggle began to figure out who would be king. This led to the selection of Philip De Valois, a nephew of the aforementioned Philip the Fair.

He would rule as Philip VI from 1328 to 1350. This would begin the Valois line, ultimately intersecting with the Capet line. There were problems from the very beginning. First, there was a rival, a strong claimant to the French crown in the form of King Edward III of England. Insecure about his own place, Valois sought to have Edward immediately recognize him. The fact that Edward dithered in doing so only made Philip all the more suspicious.

Edward himself was a young king who came to the throne at the age of 14. However, he did not achieve true power until 1337 at the age of 17. It was incidentally enough, the same year that the Hundred Years' War erupted, for it was when the young and reckless King Edward III was free of his handlers that he suddenly declared himself the rightful heir to France itself. This is what kicked off the Hundred Years' War!

It is a bit of a misnomer to call the Hundred Years' War a war since it was essentially a long series of bitter, bloody, interconnected conflicts rather than a non-stop spate of warfare. At any rate, for the sake of historical clarity, we will refer to this period of aggression between England and France as the "Hundred Years' War." The English launched the first major offensive during this war in the fall of 1339.

At this time, an army of English troops spilled into French territory and laid waste to several villages, with little or no care for the civilian populations they systematically destroyed. It was a bitter contest between the competing monarchs from the beginning. The French king was so incensed that he challenged the English king to hand-to-hand combat.

The matter, apparently, could have been settled right then and there. But to the chagrin and embarrassment of the French, after the strong and strapping English king accepted, the French king had second thoughts and backed out of the deal! In the meantime, the English received an unexpected boon in January of 1349 when the citizens of Flanders suddenly recognized Edward's claim to the crown. So it was that the war continued.

For several years, France seemed to be on the brink of complete disaster. In 1415, the English successfully destroyed the French Cavalry at Agincourt, and many more disasters would follow. In the spring of 1429, the English were on the verge of seizing the city of Orleans and the whole Loire Valley that surrounded it. They were stopped, not by the armies of the French king, but by a peasant force led by a charismatic young woman named "Joan of Arc."

Sadly enough, Joan of Arc was later captured by her enemies and burned at the stake under charges that she was a witch. Nevertheless, this instance of bravery inspired French King Charles VII to create a professional army that could finally stand up to the English. However, he had to develop a tax lobbied at the average citizen to pay the troops. This was initially called the *fouage* tax, French for a "home and hearth" tax.

The name would later change to "*taille*" which is French simply for cutting and dividing, as in cutting and dividing money. But whatever it might have been called, this tax was unpopular and initiated without even so much as consulting with the Estates General. This retooled and better-financed fighting force ultimately drove the English out.

English forces were pushed out of Paris in 1436, and ultimately out of France as a whole, with the official end of hostilities in 1453. In the aftermath of this war and turmoil, the battles that had taken place across France had left much of the nation in ruin. Writer and historian W. Scott Haine even went as far as to liken the rubble-strewn aftermath in much of France as being akin to a Hiroshima-level event.

Considering all of this destruction, France seriously needed to rebuild its infrastructure in the aftermath of the Hundred Years' War. The remodeling of France would cost a pretty penny or, as it were France, a pretty *livre.* And according to historian Roger Price, taxation in France for reconstruction jumped from 2.3 million in 1439 all the way to 5.1 million in 1482.

Both Charles VII, who reigned from 1435 to 1461, and his successor Louis XI, who reigned from 1461 to 1483, would have major rebuilding projects as an essential part of their rule. Along with building *buildings,* there was also a need to build up the civil structure of France.

Because the French government was on the brink of complete collapse during the worst of the conflict, there was a need to revive much of the natural bureaucracy of French governance. It is said that by the early 1500s, some sixteen million French citizens were administered by a bureaucracy that comprised around 4 percent of the entire population of the Kingdom of France.

Chapter 4: Changes and Rising Tensions

As the 1520s dawned, France did its best to keep its head above international waters. It then came as some surprise when shortly into this decade, war erupted between France and Italy in 1521. We must be clear, however, that when we speak of "Italy," we are doing so in a general regional sense. The actual reunification of Italy into the modern-day nation-state that we know today was still a few centuries off.

Regarding France's "Italian War" of the 1520s, we are referring to a conflict that had erupted between France and various Italian-based principalities. The French king overseeing this conflict was Francis I. King Francis was one of France's most spectacular and dynamic kings in many respects. That said, he was also an "accidental king"—at least accidental in that he only rose to the throne because his predecessor, Louis XII, had no natural heirs.

Francis I was a first cousin of King Louis and had suddenly found himself on the throne. He was not expecting it, but rather than him being unprepared, it was more like France itself was unprepared for the fresh energy and ambition that this unexpected dynamo provided. King Francis proved to be a great political and military strategist, and unlike many of his predecessors, he did not take anything for granted.

Francis came to the throne in 1515, and by the time the war with Italy had erupted, he was still in his 20s. However, the conflicts that kicked off the wars fought on the Italian peninsula had begun before he was on the throne. The first major blow between the two parties occurred in 1494 when French King Charles VIII launched an invasion of Naples. This invasion triggered a reaction from Italian allies Spain and the Holy Roman Empire.

Charles was ultimately made to remove his troops, but the experience cemented in his mind, and in the mind of many of his colleagues, the richness that could be explored in the Italian peninsula. The expedition also demonstrated just how fractured the Italian states were. These findings would lead to the French putting out further feelers to see just what they could gain by aggression in Italy.

The fighting occurred at a pivotal time in world history, just after the reformation had erupted. Interestingly enough, between two of the main antagonists in this conflict—Francis I of France and Charles V of the Holy Roman Empire—there would be quite a bit of personal animosity. This stemmed from the fact that both Francis I and Charles V were in the running to be elected Holy Roman emperor after the former emperor, Maximilian, died in 1519.

The Holy Roman Empire always selected its emperors by way of electors scattered throughout the Holy Roman Empire (basically Central Europe), and a claimant had to gain enough of them to be elected emperor. It did not matter if a claimant was already a king (as was the case with Francis I); if elected, he would have had two titles: king of France and Holy Roman emperor.

The Protestant Reformation once again came into play in the election of Charles V as Holy Roman emperor. Pope Leo was banking on Charles V's support to counteract Martin Luther and the German Protestants. Ultimately, this notion would sway Pope Leo toward backing Charles V rather than Francis I. This served to put a wedge between Francis I and Pope Leo. And shortly after Charles V was elected emperor, Francis I began aligning himself with the pope's nemesis: the Venetians.

With these lines drawn, in November of 1521, a papal and imperial-backed army managed to seize Milan. The French then tried to intervene and get Milan back. This led to armed conflict on January 9, 1522, that ended in a route of French forces that April. The following month, the situation worsened for France since England suddenly came out on the side of the papal forces and declared war against France. Spain was soon to follow.

So it was that the lines were drawn with many of Europe's leading powers suddenly moving against France's interests. France was in need of a powerful ally. This led Francis I to do what, for many Christians, must have seemed unthinkable. He sought out the support of the old foe of Christendom, the Islamic juggernaut of the Ottoman Empire.

It must be noted that Francis I was not as devout as his predecessors or many of his *successors*. He viewed the church as helpful as long as it suited his purposes, but he was not at all against aligning himself with non-Christian entities if it served his purpose. And so that is precisely what he did. Whereas his predecessors, who were still committed to the notion of Crusading against Islam, would have likely rolled over in their graves, Francis I went full steam ahead with his grand plan of hooking up with the Ottomans to offset his fellow Christian foes in Europe.

This led him to send a formal diplomatic mission to meet with Suleiman the Magnificent. However, the Ottoman Turks were not quite ready for such an ambitious and stunning arrangement and ultimately declined. They would leave the diplomatic door open, however, and eventually come out on the side of France.

In the meantime, Francis I made constant reassurances to the sultan that although at times he would make statements condemning Islam and the Turks, this was all for show. In reality, he was ready to deal.

A brief cessation of hostilities was achieved through the unexpected diplomatic wrangling of Francis' mom, Louise of Savoy, and Charles V's aunt (who happened to be Louise's sister-in-law), Margaret of Austria. These talks led to what went down in history as "the Ladies Peace," which ended hostilities on July 5, 1529. This treaty would have Francis promising to recognize Charles as being in control of Naples, Milan, as well as Artois and Flanders.

However, this would only be a brief interlude before the conflict would roar to life again. After coming out on the losing end of international conflict, Francis I turned his attention to domestic affairs. Francis was a great patron of the arts and is often considered an enlightened, renaissance-styled ruler. Francis I established a free university in France, the College de France, which would encourage learning of all kinds.

Having that said, it could very well be argued that it was due to the efforts of Francis and his college that France would later become such a hub for intellectuals. And even though there had been conflicts with

Italy, he was not hesitant to import Italian intellectuals, thereby creating the powerful cross-pollination of ideas between France and Italy that would enable a full-blown, international renaissance (or intellectual re-birth) to take shape.

But even during this enlightenment, shadows loomed large. Chief among them was France's backroom dealing with the Ottoman Empire. The Ottoman Empire was once again on the march in the spring of 1543 on land and sea. Regarding its sea offensive, the Ottomans had used their vast Mediterranean fleet to attack the shores of Italy and Sicily. This move had Francis' tacit support, but interestingly enough, it was due to Francis' request that the Papal States of Central Italy be spared and that the abode of the pope was kept safe and secure during this onslaught.

The Ottomans were initially in quiet cooperation with the French, but the dialogue would break down when the Turks became frustrated with French inaction. They wished France to join them on a terrific onslaught of Spain, but France dithered. The French ultimately offered a counterproposal, stating that they would rather launch an assault on Nice instead. The Turks did not like this but eventually agreed to the French plans. Thus, the stage was set for the siege of Nice.

The siege was launched in August 1543. To the shock of all Christendom, France was now openly siding with the Ottoman Turks. It was on the 15th of that month that the powerful canons fixed to Turkish naval craft managed to blow open the walls of Nice, and a joint force of French and Ottoman troops spilled out onto the streets of the besieged city. The city's people initially put up quite a fight, but it was useless; the French and Turkish forces overwhelmed them, and by the 22nd, Nice was in their hands.

It is said that terrible looting and pillaging followed, but it is not exactly clear whether it was the French or the Turks who were primarily to blame for these activities. Whatever the case, all of Europe was shocked at the notion that Christians, with the aid of an Islamic army, would wreak such devastation. The French were somewhat shocked by these developments; their anxieties were high when the commander of the Ottoman forces requested that his fleet and troops be allowed to overwinter in Toulon.

This meant that the French would have to be subject to what was essentially a mini-occupation of Turks on their own soil. It has been said that the Turks who were quartered in France were highly disciplined, and their commander made it clear that any Turk engaged in abusive behavior toward the locals would be severely punished. But even so, the average French citizen had been brought up to fear the Turks as the incarnation of evil itself, so one can only imagine the trepidation they must have had!

It is said that those who could relocated to other parts of France to avoid being in proximity to the Ottomans. But it seems that despite French fears, the Ottoman stay was peaceful. Nevertheless, it proved to be a heavy drain on the French economy since King Francis had to foot the bill for provisioning the guest army that had camped out on his soil. As such, Francis was eager to get the Turks out of France as soon as possible.

Turkish commander Barbarossa, finally getting the hint, had his fleet depart in April 1544. As it turns out, this engagement with the Turks would be Francis' last major international feat. Shortly after that, he grew terribly sick. In 1545, he developed a painful abscess and would linger on, significantly weakened, until March 31, 1547, when he perished at 52.

In the aftermath of Francis I's death, France had found itself adrift. The powerful and charismatic Francis was succeeded by his son Henry II. Henry was more serious about the Christian faith than his father, Francis. Rather than merely playing lip service, it is said that he was more seriously devout. Even so, he continued the strategy of France, linking up with the Ottoman Turks for extra support against the nation's erstwhile enemies in Europe.

Fighting would continue intermittently in and around the Italian peninsula until the Peace of Cateau-Cambresis was signed on April 3, 1559. Just a few months later, on July 1 of that year, Henry himself would abruptly perish during a freak accident during a friendly joust. He was jousting a younger opponent, Gabriel, Comte de Montgomery, when Gabriel's lance broke during an exchange, and a wooden splinter, shot right through Henry's visor, sliced through his eye, and then pierced into the king's brain.

He would perish in terrible pain a week later. It is worth noting that this incident is heralded as bringing the so-called French mystic and prophet, Nostradamus, to fame since he allegedly predicted it. Shortly before the incident, Nostradamus, famous for writing vague musings of all kinds, had written:

"The young lion will overcome the older one. On the battlefield in single combat. He will pierce his eyes through a golden cage. Two wounds become one, and he dies a cruel death."

Yes, on the one hand, you could write Nostradamus' words as nothing more than vague nonsense, but then again, you could find striking similarities between these musings and what actually happened to King Henry. King Henry could be said to be the old lion who was overcome by the younger man (lion) in single combat (a jousting match). And the fact that he was pierced in the eye, right through his visor (golden cage), is unmistakable.

Also, the fact that the splinter first pierced his eye (one wound) and then pierced his brain (two wounds) to create one terrible wound (two wounds become one) is also stunning to contemplate. It is also undoubtedly true that the king, who is said to have died in absolute agony days later, did indeed die a cruel death!

As it pertains to how the immediate history of France was to play out, it was after King Henry II's demise that France would undergo many dynamic and long-lasting changes. After Henry's passing, his son Francis II became king, but this Francis, unlike his robust predecessor, would have a short run of things, abruptly perishing on December 5, 1560.

He was then succeeded by his little brother Charles, who was then dubbed King Charles IX. Since he was so young, his mother, Queen Catherine de Medici, initially ruled in his stead as regent. Young King Charles IX would have a tough time due to plenty of internal discord and religious strife that had erupted in France at this time. The strife would infamously culminate in the Saint Bartholomew's Day Massacre, which erupted in Paris, France, in 1572.

This incident involved a group of French Protestants called "Huguenots" who were slaughtered in the thousands by an armed Catholic contingent. Charles IX would perish at 23 years old in 1574 with no heir. The crown would then ultimately default to Henry III, the third son of the deceased Henry II. Henry III's run would also be brief and troubled, with his own passing arriving in 1589.

The death of Henry III led to the recognition of Henry of Navarre as the new king. King Henry, subsequently dubbed Henry IV, sought to solve the religious problem by appeasing the Protestants, famously leading up to the infamous Edict of Nantes issued on April 13, 1598. Even while tackling the religious problem at home, he oversaw the expansion of French power abroad, particularly in the Americas, during his reign.

Under this king's reign, in 1608, French explorer Samuel de Champlain established the colony that would become Quebec. This allowed somewhat of a release valve to some of France's internal strife since those disenchanted with France now had the option to immigrate to this new French colony overseas. However, Henry IV's reign would end as abruptly as it had begun when he perished by assassination in 1610.

This led to the rise to the throne of the king's then nine-year-old son Louis XIII. Since he was obviously too young to rule independently, he was governed by a regency led by Marie de Medici. The most infamous member of the king's inner circle would be "Cardinal Richelieu," who served as an advisor and prime minister from 1624 to 1642. During this time, Richelieu would play a prominent role in the Thirty Years' War, which erupted in 1618.

The Thirty Years' War began as a battle of Protestantism and Catholicism but then devolved into a contest over who would dominate Europe. The conflict first erupted when the Holy Roman Empire tried to rein in some of its principalities that had turned toward Protestantism, particularly those in Bavaria which had been drifting away since the days of Martin Luther.

The Bavarians revolted, and open conflict ensued. Various sides and factions developed, and soon France was pulled into the fray. Initially, most assumed that Catholic France would join the cause of the Holy Roman Empire and its allies. But due to the insistence of Cardinal Richelieu (who, despite his ranking as a cardinal, was much keener as a political strategist than as a defender of the Catholic faith), the king of France was convinced it would be much more prudent to come out on the side of the Protestants!

Yes, the age-old hostility and fear of the Holy Roman Empire encroaching on French borders trumped religion; France found itself teaming up with the now Protestant England, the Netherlands, Bavaria, and several other Protestant-backed states against the other Catholic powers. The fighting would largely prove inconclusive as all sides hammered away at each other for several years.

Richelieu would perish in 1642 and would be followed in death by Lous XIII himself in 1643. This then led to the rise of King Louis XIV, who was only a child at the time. His regency was led by his mother, Queen Anne, and Richelieu's successor, Cardinal Giulio Mazarin. Mazarin was disliked by many in France, and he was even accused of having an affair with Queen Anne!

Making matters much worse, in 1648, Mazarin announced that the French treasury had been completely drained due to the expense of fighting the Thirty Years' War. He was only the *messenger*, but somehow wrath was aimed at him for simply conveying the message. This was especially the case when Mazarin let it be known that royal officials could not expect to receive any form of payment over the next few years while the treasury was recovering.

Soon a rebellion erupted, and the situation became so bad that Mazarin and the royal entourage had to go into hiding. Soon, negotiations were started, and a compromise with Parliament was reached, allowing the situation to return to normalcy. Mazarin perished in 1661, allowing Louis XIV to take complete control. He would prove to be an able administrator who could center all French governance around his own will.

This feat would have him dubbed the "Sun King" since, as the planets revolve around the sun, so too did the instruments of French governance revolve around Louis XIV. He seemed a natural for the task, and the fact that he would reign for a stunning 72 years indicated that he was a good fit for the job! King Louis was irreplaceably in the system of France at that time, and he knew it.

He was in fact, rather fond of stating "L' Etat, c'est moi!" Yes, imagine King Louis XIV thrusting his thumb into his chest, exclaiming, "The state is me!" Or, as we would better render it in an entirely English translation, "I am the state!"

The first signal that Louis would be an absolutist ruler was when he declared his intention of not having a Prime Minister. Gone were the days of the meddling Richelieu and Mazarin; Louis would heed only his own advice from here on out. The Estates General would not meet under his long reign, and instead of consulting others, Louis would create an elaborate system of patronage. If you genuinely wanted to have an impact on French society, consultation was no longer the means of doing so, but indulging in patronage was.

In this fashion, King Louis is said to have "pacified" the noble elites by subsidizing them, making them entirely dependent upon his benevolence. And for the rest? He kept any other potential malcontents under wraps by creating an elaborate police force to put down any sign of unrest. The first step of this new system of policing began in 1667 when King Louis created the post of lieutenant general of police in Paris.

This chief of police role was then replicated in all French cities. The lieutenant general was tasked with staying on top of keeping the peace in their district, and as soon as unrest emerged, a crackdown against it was immediately forthcoming. It has been said that the first phase of Louis' reign focused on consolidating the domestic front. With this achieved, in 1673, King Louis began to actively look outside France's borders, and much of the rest of his reign would be spent seeking pure and simple conquest.

But as had been the case before, this warfare and strife came at a steep cost. And by the end of the 17th century, France was nearly bankrupt, so much so that King Louis had to establish a new tax in 1701 called the "capitation" or poll tax, which became a routine burden on the French. Further problems, such as crop failures and disease outbreaks, would only worsen matters.

Yes, things were so bad in France that by the time the long-lived King Louis XIV passed on September 1, 1715, instead of being met with sadness, it is said that it was a cause for many average French subjects to celebrate. He was just a few days short of his 77th birthday, and instead of celebrating with a birthday bash, they celebrated the fact that he had passed!

His successor, his great-grandson Louis XV, was just a child, and Louis would prove to be a complicated leader at best and a wrong-headed one at worst. For it was under Louis XV that a series of disastrous wars, such as the War of Austrian Succession, the Seven Years' War, and the French and Indian War, would all result in French defeat and territorial losses, the latter of which would end with France losing virtually all of its territory in the Americas.

Louis XV would then be succeeded by Louis XVI, who, still smarting from his predecessor's losses, would encourage and support the Americans to rebel against France's nemesis Great Britain out of sheer spite and revenge. The ideals of the American Revolution would come back to haunt this absolutist French monarch when the same notions of

universal rights, freedom, and democracy would come home to roost in France. But the French Revolution would have nowhere near as happy an outcome as its American counterpart.

Chapter 5: The French Revolution

Upon the eruption of major world events such as the French Revolution, it is easy to immediately focus on the immediate flare-up and miss out on what led to the conflagration. Regarding the French Revolution, it would be a great disservice to neglect mention of the long stream of events that immediately preceded this watershed event.

And in doing so, we must first cast our minds back to the year 1740, when the controversy over the Austrian Succession came into play. International players squabbled over who would get their hands on the Austrian throne after the departure of Emperor Charles VI. His daughter Maria Theresa was a leading contender, supported by powerful international players such as Britain and the Dutch Republic.

However, Prussia and, ultimately, France contested her right to succeed her father. This dispute came to blows with actual physical combat. It is said that Louis XV was primarily directed to get involved by his influential minister Cardinal de Fleury and other notable ministers of his court, who argued that it would be advantageous for France to join up with the Prussians. But it most certainly was not.

France faced major defeats and setbacks. Their small victories were negated upon signing the "Treaty of Aix-la-Chapelle," ending hostilities in 1748. First of all, the main purpose of the war, the contestation of Maria Theresa to be on the throne, proved utterly useless. She was on the throne whether Prussia or France liked it or not. But much worse in the eyes of many French subjects was the fact that their king voluntarily handed over all territorial possessions he had seized during the conflict.

The French king insisted he had no use for them, stating he was the "king of France, not a merchant."

Such sentiment is perhaps more understandable today. After all, world powers today are more in the business of keeping the status quo than of world conquest. For example, the United States might have occupied Iraq and Afghanistan for various reasons, but the objective was never to permanently seize these lands to incorporate them into an American empire. But in the 1740s, world powers were indeed in the business of empire-building, and any voluntary handing over of territory was ultimately perceived as a weakness rather than a pragmatic strength.

And that was the general opinion held about King Louis XV, both in and outside France at the time. The notion that French troops had fought and struggled to gain such territory only to hand it back did not sit well with the French people. The average French subject was so dismayed that they even coined a phrase to express their disgust over what they felt was an immense struggle, fought for nothing except perhaps to aid the king of Prussia.

It was out of all of this that a French expression, which basically means that one is in the business of "working for nothing," was coined. The expression was "travailler pour le roi de Prusse." The phrase speaks of how the French had travailed (worked) so hard for the Prussian king (roi de Prusse), only to get nothing in return, and it came to be used in reference to just about any situation that seemed to qualify.

After the Austrian War of Succession ended in 1748, the French people could not help but feel as if they had been cheated. However, the worst was yet to come when the next round of international conflict erupted in 1756 at the start of the so-called "Seven Years' War." In this conflict, France came out on Austria's side and pitted itself against Britain. This destructive conflict would lead to severe setbacks in Europe, but the worst defeats would actually occur in North America, where the conflict became known by another name: the French and Indian War.

The conflict was called such because the French troops in North America had aligned themselves with local Native American tribes. In the minds of the British colonial troops, their main struggle was against the French and their Native American allies; thus, they dubbed it "the French and Indian War." But this was merely an extension of the same Seven Years' War, which had spilled over into the colonies of France and Britain.

France would come out on the losing end, and after the signing of the Peace of Paris in 1763, it lost its North American colonies in Canada to Britain. Voltaire might have once rendered the comic refrain that the king had merely lost "a few acres of snow," but it was much more serious than that. The revenue of the fur trade, which had long bolstered the French economy, was gone. And in its place was surmounting war debt.

And it was about to get worse.

Instead of consolidating the resources that France retained, King Louis XV's successor, King Louis XVI (who came to the throne in 1774), hatched a scheme to get back at the British. The means would be to use the American colonists as auxiliaries and proxies to strike out at the hated British. This dream came to fruition with the eruption of the American Revolution in 1775.

France came out on the side of the Americans, and though the French government could scarcely afford it, it helped to bankroll the American war. Thanks to French support, the Americans were indeed successful in casting off the British, but France found itself in insurmountable debt as a consequence and, once again, with next to nothing to show for it.

Perhaps it pleased the king to get revenge on the British, but the French, struggling to purchase bread and other bare essentials in the marketplace, were none too happy. Were they once again working for the king of Prussia? Or, as it were this time, were the French working for George Washington? And with absolutely nothing to show for it except inflated prices in the marketplace?

At this point, French society had reached a tipping point. The masses' discontent was palpable, and the French intelligentsia was pouring gasoline on the fire, hammering out pamphlet-after-fiery-political-pamphlet decrying the king and the general state of affairs. They also pointed out the ironic fact that the French had supported an American Revolution that threw off the English king, yet the French people were still getting around to the whims of their highly unpopular French king.

King Louis XVI certainly was not a big fan of the ideology of the American Revolution; for him, it was merely a means to an end. However, all of this would come back to bite him in a big way when the same notions of overthrowing the monarchy and establishing the French Republic became the rallying cry of the French masses. This situation was exacerbated because most taxes were being leveled at the poorer classes of French society rather than the more affluent.

Even though the more well-off French subjects often found ways to avoid taxation, the poor were relentlessly targeted with the taille tax, which would continue to be an enormous source of resentment. At this time, France's society was divided into three distinct categories or, as the French termed it, *estates.* There was the First Estate, which comprised the rich, aristocratic class, and the Second Estate, which comprised the Clergy.

Both of these classes often found a way around taxation. It was then the Third Estate, comprised of commoners who typically carried the full brunt of taxation. And all of this without much of any representation. The Estates General, the representative body meant to represent the estates, had not met in several years. It was only after great public outcry that King Louis XVI agreed to have the Estates General meet in February of 1787.

During this meeting, the king ironically heard the same rallying cry that had stirred the Americans to rebel against the king of England for he heard a unanimous shout of "no taxation without representation." King Louis was increasingly alarmed at these developments and attempted to stifle the growing outrage by suspending parliament. This backfired spectacularly when protests left the official chambers of discourse and ended up out in the street. Louis then reluctantly reconvened the Estates General on May 1, 1789.

In the meantime, the printing press of France was in overdrive, pumping out all manner of political pamphlets disparaging the French royal family and blaming them for all of the problems that the average subject of France was facing. One of the most popular pamphlets then was a work by Abbe Emmanuel Sieyes entitled "What is the Third Estate?"

After asking that question, this piece concluded that since it represented the vast bulk of the French people, the Third Estate *was the French people.* The thrust of the discourse was to encourage the French masses to rise up and claim their rights since they, the oppressed majority, were the true embodiment of the French nation. During this period, King Louis XVI seemed to follow a predictable pattern of being cowed by popular opinion, followed by his immediate alarm and attempts to crack down.

The crackdowns would then backfire, the people would be emboldened, and King Louis XVI would be further cowed and bullied. This basic pattern would repeat itself throughout the rest of King Louis XVI's troubled reign. At the outset of the Third Estate's rise to political prominence, King Louis, after calling for the Estates General to meet, grew so alarmed at what was happening that on June 20, 1789, he locked up the meeting hall so the Third Estate could not convene!

Undaunted, the Third Estate met at a public tennis court instead, where they issued their Tennis Court Oath that they would not depart until their demands, most notably a new constitution, would be met. This feat of solidarity and defiance once again cowed the king into submission, and he caved into their demands for a meeting in the National Assembly.

Once they were present at the National Assembly, declarations for establishing a "Constituent Assembly" and signing nothing short of a new constitution were made. The king, backed into a corner, felt no choice but to comply. He immediately regretted his decision and began mobilizing troops around Paris in case things turned ugly.

And turn ugly they did.

On July 14, 1789, French revolutionaries stormed the Bastille, a royal fortress/prison in Paris.

Although the storming of the Bastille is still celebrated in France, it was the start of an explosion of unbridled human emotion that would lead to some rather bloody and monstrous consequences. The storming of the Bastille was mainly done to retrieve weapons and ammunition, although the prisoners who were being kept there were also released. The guards initially held off the crowd, but once the Bastille was on the verge of being overwhelmed, those in charge agreed to hand over the fortress under the promise that their lives would be spared. They were not.

Instead of sparing the lives of those inside as promised, the mob tore them limb from limb. With bloody heads and other body parts being waved in the air by a delighted and bloodthirsty mob, the French Revolution had begun. Adding more fuel to the fire was the fact that bread prices continued to rise in the market. It may seem like a simple thing, but it was not. If prices are so inflated that the average person cannot buy food, local populations will not be content. If the problem is not solved quickly, that discontent can spill over into absolute rage.

And this was indeed what happened in France.

The king was sitting on a powder keg whether he realized it; without proper relief, his subjects were ready to let him know their desperation firsthand. This was most famously demonstrated on October 5, 1789, when a mob (led predominantly by women) marched on the king's palace in Versailles. There, all those desperate mouths desiring bread clamored that they were about to drag out the "baker, the baker's wife, and the baker's son" by force if need be.

The baker reference was a jibe at the king and his family. Sadly, plenty of people among that desperate mob were deluded enough to believe that the capture of the king would solve all of their problems. It was much simpler than that. Grabbing King Louis would certainly not ensure the poor and needy a lifetime supply of bread. But although the poor, deluded masses provided the brawn, the intelligentsia was the brains of this operation.

Several political clubs had sprung into existence. Leading the charge was a club that met in the Convent of the Jacobins, known as "Jacobins." The firebrand political ideologues of the Jacobins led the charge in stirring up the French masses as their own personal attack dogs to use against the French king. Their arguments were both complex and simple at the same time. They spoke of high-flung goals and aspirations yet dumbed things down so much that anyone could understand them when needed.

At the most simplistic level, one could imagine a Jacobin asking a hungry French mob, "You want bread?" before pointing his finger at the French king and shouting, "Well, that is the baker! Go get him!" Even worse than pointing fingers at the French king and urging mobs to attack him when it suited their purpose, the intelligentsia was not above spreading absolute lies.

After a catastrophically failed harvest in 1789, a terrible conspiracy theory known as the "Great Fear" suggested a royal and aristocratic plot in the works to kill off the peasants by deliberately destroying crops. The notion is just as ridiculous as it sounds, but as French historian and writer W. Scott Haine once put it, "in the overheated and undernourished minds of the peasantry," it seemed to work.

Lies were spread to further disparage the king and absolute fury and hatred were stoked in the hearts of the average French subject. King Louis was largely oblivious to what was happening in his kingdom and ultimately became a prisoner. He was marched off to Paris, where the revolutionaries carefully watched him.

Sick of his veritable confinement, the king and his family attempted to slip away in 1791, only to be found out and forced to turn back. From this point forward, there was no mistake; the king and his whole court were under house arrest. An arrest ended with the king's execution on January 21, 1793, and the queen's execution on October 16 of that same year.

But if the average French citizen felt that their suffering would end or that they would have an adequate supply of bread with the killing of the king and queen of France, they were mistaken. On the contrary, the lives of the average person were about to get a lot worse as the intelligentsia that had mobilized the mob began to turn on the mob itself.

When further demonstrations were held attempting to protest the dire state of the French people, the Jacobins, under the agency of the newly established Committee on Public Safety, launched a campaign of sheer terror against them. Now those people in the streets demanding bread, those who had been weaponized by the intelligentsia to use against the royal family, were suddenly dubbed as enemies of the revolution. And no matter how much they protested the inflated, high prices, complaints about bread were no longer palatable to the intelligentsia elites.

The leading architect of the terror, Jacobin giant Maximilian Robespierre, showed his utter disdain and contempt for the poor, starving masses by condemning them for having nothing better to complain about than "paltry merchandise." But in truth, most of the masses just wanted stable bread prices. The intelligentsia desired revolution and used the hungry masses as tools to get it.

The Jacobins got their revolution, but the mobs of distressed citizens they used to obtain it did not get their bread. They had been duped into "working for the king of Prussia" once again. Yet this Jacobin stand-in for the king of Prussia not only tricked them as a means to their ends, but they were also ready to dispatch with them when they no longer served their purpose.

As such, a wave of terror was launched against anyone who dared criticize or question the regime. Soon heads were being chopped off at an astonishing rate, as a climate of absolute paranoia and fear was created. The only thing that ended this terror was when Robespierre himself was executed. In the aftermath, Napoleon Bonaparte, a powerful and charismatic general, came to power.

He ultimately became the dictator of France. Lending yet another layer of irony, the French Revolution that sought to rid France of an absolutist monarch ended by establishing another, for it was in 1802 that Napoleon was made dictator as "Consul for Life." This was followed up with his being given the entirely ostentatious title of "Emperor of France" in 1804. And to add yet more insult to injury, it was declared that all of his offspring would inherit the same title!

Napoleon had just begun a new dynastic line of tyrants. Yes, the French had apparently been struggling for nothing. They had fought for the king of Prussia and gained nothing for their efforts. No bread, no end to the monarchy, nothing for their trouble but Napoleon Bonaparte and a series of protracted warfare that would erupt across Europe and beyond.

Chapter 6: The Napoleonic Wars

Although Napoleon looms large in French history, he was actually a native of Corsica, which was not acquired by France until 1768. Ironically, if France had never taken over the little island of Corsica, it is highly likely that Napoleon Bonaparte would never have become the emperor of France. Perhaps emperor of a small Mediterranean island, but France? Not likely!

Regarding the governance of France itself, Napoleon first came to prominence in the aftermath of the terror when a so-called "Directory" was established to restore order. One of the members of the director was French General Paul Barras. Napoleon was in good with Barras, and through him, he gained increased influence in French governmental affairs. Napoleon had returned to France fresh from foreign battles, only to be called upon by the Directory to put down a revolt deemed "counterrevolutionary."

Napoleon used his soldiers to put down the unrest and was made the "Commander of the Army of the Interior." Napoleon was then given the authority to send his soldiers door-to-door to seize weapons. Ironically enough, all of the weapons pilfered from French garrisons (such as the Bastille) at the outset of the revolution were now being seized and taken from the citizens! With internal unrest stabilized, Napoleon once again led French forces abroad, just in time to take on the latest coalition of international forces that had risen against France.

Napoleon stifled the Italians at Piedmont in the spring of 1796, then marched on Austria, forcing them into a peace treaty on October 17,

1797. This involved the dismantling of the Republic of Venice. Among the many policies that Napoleon shattered, this was one of the longest-lived, stretching back over a thousand years. Yet, Napoleon was able to bully the Venetians into being divided between the French and the Austrians as part of the Treaty of Campo Formio.

With the Austrian and Italian fronts secure, the only bane of Napoleon's existence to remain was that of England. Initially, an amphibious assault on Britain was considered, but it did not take long for Napoleon and his colleagues to realize the impossibility of such a feat. The British had the best navy in the world at the time, and France's tattered naval vessels did not stand much of a chance.

It was in light of all this that Napoleon and company considered an alternative; if they could not put a dent in England by crossing the English Channel, they would instead cross the Mediterranean. Napoleon sent a French fleet to Egypt to take on British interests in the region. Britain was heavily involved in trade here, and it was believed that Egypt could serve as a stepping stone to the crown jewel of the British Empire: India.

With this in mind, the French launched across the Mediterranean to Egypt. Before they landed off the Egyptian coast, however, they first made a pitstop in Malta, where Napoleon saw to it that he ruined and dismantled yet another ancient order, none other than the Knights Hospitaller. The Hospitaller Knights had been holed up in Malta since the Crusades.

Napoleon decided to forcibly disband them and seize their island. He now had Malta as a base of operations right in the middle of the Mediterranean. It was after this that he and his troops headed off to Egypt. This was not the first time in history that a French army had invaded Egypt. The same feat had been attempted by Saint Louis himself during the 7th Crusade. But although the action was being repeated, the motives and cast of characters had significantly changed.

This was by no means a religious crusade. And Napoleon was not a Christian crusader. On the contrary, upon reaching the gates of Alexandria, he had interpreters proclaim to the stunned Egyptians that he respected Mohammad and Islam and was there to free them from the Mameluke warriors that had recently taken control of the nation.

Napoleon had gotten this idea that he could break the Mameluke's hold of Egypt and repatriate Egypt back to the Ottoman Empire, which had since lost much of any real control over the region. Napoleon proclaimed as much, but the locals were either not keen to be returned to the sultan, or they did not care too much for French invaders suddenly dropping down in their backyard.

Either way, the locals were sure to give Napoleon and company as hard a time as they possibly could. And no matter how much he might have stressed that he was "on their side," no one seemed to believe it. Nevertheless, Napoleon successfully seized Alexandria, making it a new forward base of operations. From here, Napoleon's forces would launch an assault on Cairo. The struggle for Cairo would occur on July 21, 1798, and go down in history as the "Battle of the Pyramids."

At this point, Napoleon may have seemed rather ingenious, but there was a coalition of European powers forming against him—the second coalition, to be exact. As it turns out, the Russians were quite miffed over what had happened in Malta. Tsar Paul had been an honorary grand master of the Hospitallers; soon, Russia was getting involved. The War of the Second Coalition would have England and Russia team up against the French. And as much as Napoleon dreamed of becoming the best friend of the Ottomans, they ended up throwing in their lot with the Second Coalition as well.

The forces of the Second Coalition and the French engaged each other in the summer of 1799 as they duked it out in the Netherlands. The French had some Dutch allies on hand as they attempted to repel the coalition forces from Holland. After sustaining heavy casualties, the Coalition force was ultimately forced to flee after the Battle of Castricum on October 6, 1799.

Napoleon had just returned from his misadventure in Egypt (a costly one that saw the French fleet smashed by British Admiral Horatio Nelson) and found France again suffering from internal discord and turmoil. Napoleon, seeking to restore order, used the men under his command to forcibly seize power on November 9, 1799.

He was made First Consul of France, which essentially made him the dictator of the whole nation. Shortly after this rank was achieved, Napoleon engaged Coalition forces on June 14, 1800, at the Battle of Marengo in northern Italy. The Coalition forces were ultimately defeated, and the French gained complete control of Italy.

Napoleon returned to France in triumph, and just a couple of years later, in 1802, he was made Consul for Life. This was then followed by his being hailed as emperor in 1804. That same year, Napoleon rolled out his own civil code (later known as the Napoleonic Code), which codified into law many of the ideals of the Revolution, albeit with the authoritarian force of Napoleon behind them.

This civil code made sure that some semblance of equality was given to French citizens and established a meritocracy in which one could rise through the ranks of French society by virtue of their own particular skills rather than through birth or by merely buying their way into a guild, as had been all too common in the past. Even after Napoleon was long gone, establishing this civil code would be one of his most lasting legacies.

France and Britain had temporarily called a truce due to the signing of the Treaty of Amiens in 1802. This temporary ceasefire had already broken down shortly after Napoleon was crowned emperor in 1804. As beaten and battered as their navy already was, the French began to challenge the British on the high seas as thoughts again turned to the idea of an invasion of Britain.

But once the British smashed the French ships at Cape Finisterre in July of 1805 and trounced the French Navy at Trafalgar a short time later, all plans to invade Britain by sea were shelved. Instead, Napoleon revamped his warfare over land; striking out at the Coalition army assembled at Austerlitz, he dealt the Austrian and Prussian armies a terrible blow that December.

And even though the British were just out of reach, Napoleon embarked upon a strategy of economic warfare. Consolidating his control over the European continent, he sought to exclude the British from all trade by instituting his "Continental System." He hoped he could choke Britain of essential resources, but Britain's robust trade still managed to get through several holes in Napoleon's system.

One of those holes was Russia, which, although not at war with Napoleon, proved to only half-heartedly comply with Napoleon's Continental policy. This led Napoleon to make plans for an invasion of Russia itself. This disastrous invasion was launched in June of 1812. Napoleon had cobbled together a large army of some 600,000 troops at this point, and if he could face off with Russian forces in open combat, he had a good chance of victory.

However, the Russian commanders in the field were smart enough to deprive Napoleon of this opportunity. Instead of facing him in open combat, they carefully withdrew, leading Napoleon further and further into Russia. As the Russian armies departed, they deployed a scorched earth policy, burning everything behind them as they fled. This was done so that Napoleon's conquering armies would find nothing to help sustain them.

They then fought a terrible battle with Russian troops near Moscow. The French were victorious but at the cost of some seventy thousand dead French troops. The Russian army was not defeated; it merely decided to withdraw farther east. Napoleon made it all the way to Moscow, only to find it virtually abandoned and burned to a crisp! As such, he could not supply his troops, and as the harsh Russian winter set in, they were in for a terrible time as the soldiers could barely keep warm and faced the threat of frostbite.

There was also the problem of random attacks by the few citizens who hung around the city. They could trust no one, had no food, and could barely keep warm. To his chagrin, Napoleon realized that although he was occupying the Russian capital, with the Russian army lurking in the far eastern frontier of the nation, he could not say that he had conquered Russia.

Instead, he was forced to flee from his illusory conquest and send his freezing, starving troops on a humiliating and deadly march back to France. As soon as they turned tail and ran, the Russian army came out from hiding in the east and mercilessly harassed the fleeing French soldiers. Tens of thousands of French soldiers lost their lives; many simply froze to death.

It is said that this terrible episode marked the second time that Napoleon abandoned his troops since he hopped on a fast sled back to France while the rest of his army slowly and painfully slogged their way back home on foot. As in Egypt, Napoleon arrived back in Paris to do damage control before word of his terrible defeat became widely known.

It did not matter; the writing was already on the wall. And after another disastrous loss to the coalition at Leipzig in October of 1813, Napoleon knew it was over. He ultimately sued for peace in the spring of 1814 and abdicated on April 4. In the terms of the subsequent agreement, the Treaty of Fontainebleau, France was stripped of its empire, and Napoleon himself was exiled to a tiny island called "Elba" in the middle of the Mediterranean.

Louis XVIII, the brother of the deceased Louis XVI, was placed on the French throne. France seemed to have come full circle; the monarchy that so many heads had rolled over was back in force. But this, of course, was not the end of the story. Napoleon would stage a great escape from his island prison and, for one hundred heady days, would lead France once again.

On February 26, 1815, Napoleon managed to sneak on board a French brig called *L'Inconstant* and land in mainland France on March 1. News of his escape had already gotten out, and a French army was sent to apprehend the fugitive former emperor. But in one of Napoleon's most memorable moments, rather than run from these troops sent to seize him, he ran toward them.

It is said that he opened up his coat and dared the incoming troops to shoot him on the spot. Napoleon supposedly shouted, "If any of you would shoot his Emperor, here I am!" Instead of shooting or even simply arresting the dictator, the troops broke out into spontaneous cheers! Just like that, Napoleon was back in charge of one of Europe's most powerful armies.

In retrospect, it might seem predetermined that Napoleon's troops would celebrate him this way. But if we were to truly consider the mood and atmosphere of France at the time, this gamble that Napoleon made was *far from certain*. Yes, many were indeed upset with the return of the old French monarchy, the loss of empire, and the general feeling of being bullied by other European powers, but at the same time, many among the French were quite frustrated with Napoleon himself.

Some did not hesitate to blame him for France's recent miseries. One of the former French marshals, Michel Ney, had, just before Napoleon's return, gone on the record to state that he felt that Napoleon should be held responsible for many of France's problems and even went as far as to state that Napoleon "should be brought back in an iron cage."

Yet, after Napoleon returned, most began singing a different tune - *literally*. They were singing the song of "Vive l' Empereur!" and there was suddenly hope that Napoleon would somehow reverse the recent misfortunes of France.

But it was not to be.

Foreign powers refused to even recognize Napoleon as a legitimate leader at this point, and on March 25, 1815, yet another coalition of Britain, Russia, Austria, and Prussia came into being to stop Napoleon in his tracks.

This coalition would render Napoleon's final defeat in the Battle of Waterloo, which took place that June. Napoleon was forced to flee back to Paris with what remained of his shattered army. There, he once again stepped down as ruler of France, abdicating on June 22. He attempted to slip away once again as the coalition forces closed in, but he found all of the ports blocked.

Knowing there was nowhere to run and not wanting to be hunted down like a dog, Napoleon decided to turn himself over to the British. Napoleon surrendered on July 15 and was soon on a British ship to head off to his next destination in exile: the island of St. Helena. He would spend his final days here until he perished on May 5, 1821.

Chapter 7: The Long 19th Century

It was only after Napoleon was deposed for good that King Louis XVIII got a firm grip on the French throne. Louis and his regime were initially quite good at balancing the royalist faction in France with the new class of notables that had emerged since the French Revolution. One of the critical architects in this balancing act was the king's minister, Elie Decazes.

The king, while being part of the royal restoration, made sure to abide by a new charter that recognized most of the democratic gains of the revolution. Much of the same promised freedoms that the French Revolution claimed to endorse would also be protected and supported by the French king. His reign would last until 1824, when due to a wide variety of afflictions, including gout and even a bout of gangrene, he perished on September 16 of that year.

This marked the final time in history when a French king would perish while still in power. Upon his passing, the "Comte d' Artois" would be tapped to succeed him as King Charles X. Charles X was another older king; he was already 67 years old when he was crowned. Despite his age, he seemed to lack the wisdom many hoped he might bring to the throne.

Instead, he seemed to be a man stuck in the past. Whereas his predecessor Louis XVIII was keenly aware of the changes that had been made to French society and had sought to adapt and compromise royal protocols to go along with it, Charles seemed as if he wanted to roll back all of the gains of the revolution and return to an absolute monarchy.

The first signal that this was the case came on May 29, 1825, when Charles X was crowned at Reims Cathedral in an elaborate and ostentatious display, which had not occurred since the days of the Ancien Régime. Needless to say, this would not sit well with the French people. Even so, Charles X proved to be quite an adventurist. In much the same way as Napoleon, his exploits overseas served as a great distraction to the problems occurring at home.

For it was in July of 1830 that he directed French forces to engage in an expedition in Algeria. Soon the French flag was flying over Algeria, and the French would occupy this piece of North African real estate for over a century, not officially exiting until 1962. As much of a distraction, as these external developments might have provided, it could not prevent the continuing internal discord from finally showing through.

King Charles X had already made moves to suspend the constitution, and that July, he worked to censor what had previously been a free press. Since the notion of a free press and the rights promised in the constitution were central to the gains of the French Revolution; those against a return of absolutist monarchy were naturally aghast. The question was what was anyone going to do about it.

As for the printing presses, it is said that in one example, after an official showed up with some personnel to dismantle one of them, as soon as he left the scene, those same workers put it right back together in complete defiance of what they had just been ordered to do. Even more ominous for the regime was when a massive group of protesters showed up just outside the Palais-Royal, demanding their rights to be recognized.

With memories of such things as the storming of the Bastille not that far removed from history at this point, it seemed that just about anything could happen. The fears of officials in charge of keeping the peace were also exacerbated by the fact that the best legions of French troops were down in Algeria. Having that said, if there was indeed a major uprising, it would have been difficult to put down.

Making matters even worse, many of the soldiers stationed in France began to defect over to the protesters. In what would have basically been a repeat of the French Revolution that saw many of the royal troops join in with demonstrators, it was quite clear that Charles X only had one thing left to do: resign. Literally resigned to his fate, Charles X put in his resignation on August 2, 1830.

Shortly after that, he and his whole family left France to go into their self-imposed exile in England. His cousin, the duke of Orleans, Louis Philippe, succeeded him. Louis Philippe, the "citizen king," positioned himself not so much as the king of France but as the king of the French. He promised that he would be the standard bearer for the rights of the revolution that they so desperately craved.

He would respect the constitution and the freedom of the press and do his best to uphold the dignity of the French people, or so he claimed. His domestic strategy was to uphold the rights of the French, while his international strategy was to have close and strong alliances while avoiding unnecessary foreign entanglements. Bucking the tradition of centuries of animosity, the closest international ally that King Philippe sought out was Britain.

He most wished to emulate Britain in forming a constitutional monarchy, in which compromise and consideration of the public good was key. But no matter how much Philippe hoped he could find a winning balance of stability, it was not the case. Instead, his tenure as king was quite turbulent. He may have avoided outright revolution, but there were several episodes of protests, demonstrations, and even outright insurrections.

He also had to routinely shuffle the deck of his ministers. It is said that from August of 1834 to February of 1835, he went through five prime ministers. He also just barely dodged an assassination attempt on July 28, 1835. He was traveling from Tuileries to look at the National Guard, only to get shot at by a gunman who fired on him from a window of a nearby building. Even though the king escaped harm, several people were mowed down in the melee of bullets that tore into his entourage. This would not be the last attempt on Philippe's life, and he would face an assassin's attempt again in June of 1836.

In the meantime, Louis Napoleon, the nephew of Napoleon Bonaparte (who would later be dubbed "Napoleon III"), had been stirring up trouble. Using his name to provoke the Bonapartists, he attempted a coup in 1835 and tried again in 1840 before fleeing to Britain. When a series of uprisings and revolutions rocked much of Europe in 1848, Napoleon III found the perfect opportunity to return. No sooner than Philippe had abdicated from the throne on February 24, 1848, Napoleon III began to make waves again in France.

A provisional government was established, and an election for who would be the president of the "Second Republic" was launched. Napoleon III threw his hat in the ring and won in a landslide. He had excellent name recognition, of course, and thanks to the distance of several years between them and the events of the Napoleonic Wars, the hearts of many in the French public had grown rather fond of the old Bonaparte. The disasters that Napoleon Bonaparte had brought upon France during his reign were much forgotten, and those who wished to see the past through rose-colored glasses only remembered the prestige and greatness of Bonaparte.

It was these longings to be great once again that they projected onto the shoulders of his nephew Louis-Napoleon. And Louis, or as he preferred to be called, "Napoleon III," was ready to accept the expected mantle. Shortly after his election, he made sure to celebrate in the Elysée Palace, where his famous uncle had taken up residence in the past. Although perhaps many had empire-building on their minds when they considered the name of Napoleon, the first thing on Napoleon III's plate was not the building of an empire but the consolidation of what France already had.

His most pressing obligation was to fix the faltering French economy and the failing infrastructure. And in this feat, Napoleon III was surprisingly well suited for the task. It is said that under his tenure, France, which had been previously lagging behind its European counterparts, saw the ramping up of massive industrialization. Most importantly, Napoleon III saw new rail lines laid out throughout France. The fact that France finally acquired reliable, modern railroad transportation greatly impacted the French economy.

Now that goods could be easily transported from one part of the country to another, trade and commerce flourished. Wine in southern France, for example, could be easily shipped up to Paris, creating a veritable wine boom that did not exist before. There was no longer any need for local markets for wine when France's best wine could be shipped up from sunny, southern France any day of the week.

Railroad building, and other industrialization projects, were also positive developments as far as investment banks were concerned since they suddenly had a clearly defined field in which to invest their money. Investment banks' success led to an increase in general confidence in the banks, and more and more French citizens were putting both their faith and their money in banking institutions. Banknotes now had the complete confidence of the French people, and paper currency became the standard in France. All of these things were very important for the future of France and signaled many more positive things to come.

Perhaps due to his seemingly great economic and domestic success, when Napoleon III launched a coup in December of 1851 (to stay in power indefinitely), most of the French people seemed to take it all in stride. The only real pushback came from Napoleon III's former political opponent Victor Hugo, who led small demonstrations in Paris, but these were ultimately put down by Napoleon's troops and came to absolutely nothing.

The Second Republic had been rather quickly transformed into Napoleon III's personal empire. Such a thing should have been startling, but as long as the economy was booming, there would not be too many out in the streets to protest. On the contrary, Napoleon III did everything he could to present himself not as a tyrant but as the so-called "sovereign of the people." He was, in essence, a populist leader attempting to position himself as a man of the people with their best interests at heart.

Most seemed to be convinced that this was the truth. And even if they were not, Napoleon's rapidly expanding network of secret police likely would have made short work of them. As fine-tuned as the economy and domestic affairs seemed to be under Napoleon III, that is not to say that there were not any hiccups along the way. For it was in 1867 that the French lending institution, Credit Mobilier, failed.

But besides the banking collapse of Credit Mobilier, the worst setback that Napoleon III would face was his foreign policy. First, in 1862, during the height of the American Civil War, he backed a reckless expedition into Mexico, which installed Austrian Archduke Maximillian as the emperor of Mexico in 1864. This was supposedly done in retaliation for loans the Mexican government had failed to repay.

It is certainly not good for a country to fail in paying its debt, but most, then and now, would consider military occupation over defaulted loans a rather extreme choice to remedy the situation. And shortly after the Civil War ended, with the U.S. government no longer distracted by internal discord, France was told in no uncertain terms to keep its hands off of Mexico. This resulted in French troops leaving in 1867, even though Maximillian and his entourage attempted to stay, resulting in his arrest and death by firing squad.

Napoleon III likely wanted to put this debacle behind him quickly. But more failed foreign policy was to come. Since France had declared neutrality after the outbreak of hostilities between Prussia and Austria in 1866, they had been pulled ever closer to war with Prussia itself, a war that would erupt as the "Franco-Prussian War" in July of 1870. Napoleon III would prove to be disastrously unprepared for the masterful strategy of the Prussian leader Otto von Bismarck.

Napoleon would lose this war when on September 2, 1870, he and some eighty-four thousand soldiers were made to surrender after losing the Battle of Sedan. After this military defeat, Napoleon III finally faced personal defeat as leader of France. He was deposed, the empire was rendered null and void, and the French declared the coming of a Third Republic.

But even though France no longer referred to itself as an empire, it had enough sprawling territory to be considered imperial in scope. Despite its defeat in Europe, during the reign of Napoleon III, France had acquired considerable overseas territory. On the African continent, Algeria and Senegal had both become French colonies. The French took over modern-day Vietnam, Cambodia, and Laos in Southeast Asia, creating French Indo-China.

During this period, France also engaged in a pseudo-crusade by sending French troops to Lebanon, supposedly to protect Maronite Christians and Christian places of worship. Yes, France may no longer have called itself an Empire after the downfall of Napoleon III, but the imperial ambitions that France still projected onto much of the world at the end of the 19th century were indeed quite clear

Chapter 8: France's Long March toward the Guerre de Revanche

The Franco-Prussian War ended in a humiliating defeat. The National Assembly of France, which served as the acting authority of the nation at the time, signed its armistice with Prussia on January 28, 1871. This ended the Franco-Prussian War, but the bleak terms of the agreement would spark tremendous internal discord in France itself. The treaty had France lose European territories such as Alsace and Lorraine and had France fork out billions of francs in reparations.

However, the worst was yet to come when it was announced that the National Assembly would discontinue the salaries of the National Guardsmen stationed in Paris. The unrest of these harsh terms ignited massive protests in the streets of Paris and ultimately led to the Paris Commune, which came into spontaneous existence in March of 1871. The commune itself would be defended by those same National Guard troops who had been denied their paychecks.

The commune was a short-lived social experiment that would be forcefully put down that May. From March to May, Paris became a besieged encampment in which the Parisians (who had previously benefited from the railcars that regularly brought goods to the city) were forced to make do with whatever they had on hand. This led to dreadful scenes in which people in the city made meals out of cats, dogs, and sometimes even captured rats.

During these lean months, even the local zoo was not immune to the hunger of the demonstrators; at some point, even a couple of elephants were procured and butchered to supply meat for the besieged Parisians. On May 21, 1871, the loyal federal forces closed in, and the "bloody week" began, which saw the French regular army engage the National Guardsmen and their fellow revolutionaries, leading to the deaths of tens of thousands.

Although the commune was put down, its spontaneous eruption would leave a lasting impact on the likes of Karl Marx, who himself would later be considered the founder of *communism.* In his later writings on the subject, Marx considered the Paris Commune an example of a spontaneous eruption of what he called the "Dictatorship of the Proletariat." Marx viewed this event as an example of what might happen if the proletariat, or the average person on the street, took control of the government.

The threat of the commune allowed for the rise of French politician Adolph Thiers, who restored order and then took on the position of president and premier of the new French Republic. From this post, he managed to mitigate losses, and through the strategic use of so-called "loan drives," he was able to pay off 5 billion dollars' worth of reparations way ahead of schedule.

It was in 1872 that Thiers then set about remaking the French Republic in the most conservative image he could imagine. He reasoned that the French were tired of radical revolts, and the time for a restoration of the conservative status quo was in order. This was, in many ways, a return to the more conservative populism of Napoleon III, except without his imperial pretensions.

In many ways, French society has shifted back and forth between these two modes of thought since the days of the French Revolution. The French Revolutionaries were driven by the far left, only for a conservative backlash executed by Napoleon Bonaparte to come about. The revolutionaries of 1848 then led to much the same reaction by the factions of France championed by Napoleon III.

That said, the temporary uprising of the Commune of Paris can be viewed as the pendulum ever so briefly swinging back to the left before Adolph Thiers quickly turned it back to the right. By 1873, Thiers had been succeeded by Marshal MacMahon as president, who would remain so until he was forced to resign in 1879. Although ostensibly the "president" of the Republic, MacMahon was imbued with enough influence and power by France's monarchist faction, that many viewed him as a kind of uncrowned monarch.

Nevertheless, when a Republican majority was elected in the French Senate in 1879, he was indeed forced from power. Following the ouster of MacMahon, this particular spate of republican rule would last all the way until the year 1898. During this period, the infamous Dreyfus Affair erupted. The ordeal began in 1894 when an army officer named Alfred Dreyfus was accused of espionage, ultimately convicted, and exiled to Devil's Island.

However, even as those on the right congratulated themselves for a job well done, those on the left began to rail against the conviction as nothing short of political persecution at best and outright antisemitism at worst. Leading this charge was writer and activist Emile Zola. Zola's paper, *I accuse*, laid the case for what he believed to have been the framing of Dreyfus.

The arguments continued back and forth between the liberal left and the conservative right until Dreyfus was ultimately exonerated in 1906. The world was going through many changes, and alliances were shifting. By 1907, France had entered into the Triple Entente, in which France was firmly allied with Britain and Russia. This alliance was made to counteract what French officials viewed as the growing threat of Germany.

The German Empire had been declared after France had come out on the losing end of the Franco-Prussian War. Many are unaware of this fact, but the modern nation of Germany, as we know it today, did not exist until then. Before this, various German confederations and principalities existed in conglomerations such as the Holy Roman Empire and Prussia, but there was no "Germany."

It was in the aftermath of France's defeat that a unified German state was declared. Almost immediately, the new robust German nation on France's borders, which saw rapid increases in its military and economy, was a tremendous point of concern and anxiety for the French. As such, the French sought reassurance by entering into an alliance with Britain and Russia in case the Germans caused them any trouble. But as much as the French believed that this alliance brought them assurance, it also brought tremendous entanglement.

For not only were Britain and Russia obligated to come to France's aid, but France was also obligated to come to its partners' aid as well. This ensured that France could potentially be embroiled in conflicts with little or nothing to do with its own interests. And with the outbreak of World War I in 1914, this is more or less what happened. What interest did France have in declaring war on Germany simply because of German saber-rattling in the Balkans?

Yet, after one isolated incident in which a Serbian nationalist assassinated an Austrian duke, France was pulled into what would become World War One. The duke was killed, Austria made harsh demands, and when Serbia refused to meet them, Germany backed Austria's desire for reprisal. Russia, seeking to aid the Serbs, stood up to Germany. France was therefore obligated to stand up to Germany as well.

As the situation continued to spiral out of control, the lines of World War One would be drawn with the allies of Britain, France, and Russia, waging war against the so-called Central Powers of Germany, Austria, and the Ottoman Empire. As sudden as all of this was, some in France welcomed these developments. There was a movement known as the League of Patriots in particular, who had been clamoring for what they called "Guerre de Revanche" (a War of Revenge) to reclaim some of the prestige France had lost in 1870.

Yes, for some in France, their memories of past grievances were long, and even several decades later, the war erupting in 1914 seemed like an ample enough opportunity to reclaim lost ground. At the outset, the Allies and the Central Powers hoped for a quick and decisive war. But ultimately, the war would drag on in a bloody stalemate over the next few years.

The Germans had attempted to strike a lethal blow to the French by overrunning the low countries, driving through Belgium, and entering northern France. The goal was to push through all the way to Paris, but the French and their Allies successfully halted the German advance at the "Battle of the Marne." The Germans, it seems, underestimated the French fighting spirit. Although much of the French infrastructure had been damaged in the German drive south, the French troops had high morale and were determined to defend Paris. As such, they ferociously fought off the Germans.

Although the Germans would remain entrenched in northeastern France, thanks to the steadfast determination of the French army, they would not proceed any further. It was here on the so-called "Western Front" that much of the rest of this bloody war would be fought. The war would be fought hunkered down in the trenches with little to no change in territorial gains. Even so, the fighting was terrible and, at times, punctuated by poison gas. At the Battle of Ypres in April 1915, the Germans deployed poison gas against their enemies on the Western Front.

The next turning point of the war came with the bloody Battle of Verdun in 1916. The French troops were led by General Philippe Petain, who would later rise to infamy as the leader of Vichy France. However, during this period, he was the heroic leader of the French resistance to German aggression. Petain was a marvel of energetic action as he mobilized his troops in a seemingly non-stop effort to repel the Germans.

The French ultimately succeeded in this objective, but their victory came at a high cost of life. The war would drag on until the United States entered, eventually forcing the German front to collapse outright. The war finally ended with the singing of an armistice on November 11, 1918. This led to the Treaty of Versailles, which attempted to carve out the postwar order as the Allies saw fit.

According to this agreement, the French would see the repatriation of the Alsace-Loraine region that it had lost in the Franco-Prussian War. If this was the reward received for the Guerre de Revanche for many French, especially those who fought in the trenches, it must have seemed rather hollow.

For the Germans, the results would be even more bitter; Germany was militarily neutered, socked with heavy reparations, and subjected to the French occupation of the Rhineland. It was all of this bitterness that would serve as a prelude and sow the seeds for the next world war to come.

Chapter 9: La Resistance and Failing Colonialism

The seeds for World War Two had been planted shortly after the cessation of World War One. The war's end had left a bitter taste in the mouth of many who fought it, French and Germans included. The French at least could try and rationalize the tremendous loss of life with the notion that they had "won" the war. For the Germans, however, there was no such solace, only a sense of humiliated defeat.

It was these bitter feelings that Hitler and his Nazi party nourished as they gained prominence in the 1920s and then further reinforced when Hitler came to power in 1933. The French were well aware of the renewed German threat that they faced, but French leadership proved incredibly indecisive in how to deal with it. Even after Germany had rearmed and forcibly marched back into the Rhineland in March of 1936, neither the French nor their British allies did much of anything about it.

This hesitation to act only emboldened Hitler and his Nazis to become even more aggressive. There was a general desire among both the French and the British to avoid war, but the appeasement that resulted would ultimately bring about the very war that they were trying so hard to avoid. An emboldened Hitler began arbitrarily annexing nearby territories such as Austria and Czechoslovakia.

It was only when Hitler invaded Poland in 1939 that the British and the French were finally compelled to declare war on Germany. Germany then launched its blitzkrieg in May of 1940, which had German tanks rolling over the low countries of Belgium, Luxembourg, and the Netherlands, before penetrating into France.

The French were woefully unprepared for this onslaught and informed the British as much. The British, fearing French collapse, were ultimately forced to evacuate the forces they had in France. This led to the evacuation of hundreds of thousands of British troops from Dunkirk, France, as German troops closed in. France ultimately surrendered to Germany that June and ushered in what was referred to as the "Third Republic of France."

However, it was much more complicated than that since France was now essentially a divided nation. The Germans took over northern and western France outright, leaving only a rump state centered around Vichy. This new incarnation of France, subsequently dubbed "Vichy France," would be led by that ironclad French general of the First World War, Marshal Philippe Petain.

Although the Vichy government declared itself neutral, it was often enough coerced into being an active collaborator of the Nazis. The Nazis also successfully turned French sentiment against their former British allies. After the French fleet was destroyed by the British at the port of Mers El Kebir, for example, the Germans were able to use this as a propaganda club with which to hit the British over the head.

The British feared the Germans might get their hands on the French fleet, so they ordered the French to decommission their ships. When the French refused, the British launched an unprovoked attack against the French navy, blowing the French vessels out of the water. Obviously, this British attack was on a former ally and did not do much to improve relations with the French.

Nevertheless, French exiles in England had to somehow put such things behind them as they rallied toward the cause of "Free France." This movement of French exiles led by Charles de Gaulle would play a crucial role in the eventual liberation of France. So too, would the French resistance in France itself. The resistance of occupied France first conducted small-scale sabotage, such as destroying railroad tracks and phone cables. But after linking up with official contacts in Britain and among the Free French, a steady stream of both arms and intelligence allowed a truly underground army of resistance to form.

In the meantime, the Germans had severely overplayed their hand, despite their seemingly easy victories over Norway, the low countries, France, and Poland. They were about to suffer from two strategic blows that would prove lethal. First, the German army invaded Russia. After rolling over Poland, the German high command somehow convinced itself that an invasion of Russia would be a walk in the park and launched the ill-fated Operation Barbarossa in June of 1941.

Seemingly forgetting all of the lessons of history, in particular, one learned by French dictator Napoleon himself, invading Russia's massive, frozen expanse is a formidable challenge logistically alone and likely doomed to failure. If this was not bad enough, Germany's ally Japan decided to attack Pearl Harbor, Hawaii, in December of 1941. This brought the United States into the war, not just against Japan but also against its partner, Germany.

The Germans, who previously only had England to worry about, now had both the United States and the Soviet Union fully committed to the war. The U.S. initially wanted to charge headlong into the German forces of mainland Europe by landing on the European continent in 1942. However, the British persuaded them not to do so and to strike out against the lower-hanging fruit of Axis power in North Africa.

This led to the Americans invading much of the North African territory of Vichy France, in Morocco, Algeria, and Tunisia. With the attack at Mers El Kebir still fresh in their minds, the naval forces of Vichy France were not exactly friendly to this incursion on their territory. Although the landings in Morocco faced little resistance, it is said that Algeria, in particular, had heavy pushback from the French stationed there.

Even so, the Allies prevailed and captured Vichy France Admiral Francois Darlan. Darlan proved a strategic boon because he agreed to work with the Allies toward a ceasefire of North African Vichy France forces as long as he was recognized as "High Commissioner for France and West Africa." Supporting Darlan, a clear collaborator, was not the most palatable of choices to have to make, but it was deemed to be important enough to do so.

Even so, many Free French leaders, including Charles De Gaulle, despised this decision. But Darlan, as fate would have it, would not have long in his tenure as High Commissioner since he was assassinated on December 24, 1942. The death of Darlan opened the door for De

Gaulle to position himself as the leader of Free France, with a new base of operations established in Algeria.

The fact that a free French government had come into existence with the backing of the Allies on what was then technically French territory was a great propaganda victory for Free France. However, the Germans were not taking these developments lightly and had already moved to occupy France outright before the year was out.

Nevertheless, their stay would be brief.

The Allies eventually pulled off a successful landing in Normandy, France, on June 6, 1944, and the Free French led by Charles De Gaulle were right behind this liberation force. And this was not the end of the story as it pertains to the contributions made by the French troops during World War Two. The Free French and their allies from the underground would continue to battle the Germans all the way back to Germany, and as a result, upon Germany's defeat in 1945, the French would have their own occupied sector, along with the British, the Americans, and the Russians.

Not long after the war was over, one of these allies, the Russians, would be at odds with the rest, and a so-called Cold War between the communist East and the capitalist West would begin. The Soviet hold over East Germany would inspire the French, British, and Americans to combine their control sectors to unify into one Western German occupation zone.

France was having all kinds of problems with its faltering colonial holdings. Tensions were rising both in Algeria in North Africa, as well as in French Indochina in Southeast Asia. But of these locales, French holdings in Southeast Asia were the most pressing. French Indochina had actually been seized by the Japanese during the war. Japan was defeated along with its German and Italian allies, yet even after the Japanese were forced out, a local independence movement led by Ho Chi Minh was not about to let the French get back control.

Hi Chi Minh and his fellow cohorts in North Vietnam used communism as their vehicle to throw off the shackles of French colonialism. With the support of the Soviet Union and communist China, the Viet Minh of the north rallied at the Battle of Dien Bien Phu in 1954 and soundly defeated the French. This resulted in an agreement that had Vietnam split at the 17th parallel in recognition of communist North Vietnam and the newly established "Republic of Vietnam" in the south.

French Prime Minister Pierre Mendes-France realized that the days of French colonialism were numbered; as such, he laid out the groundwork for severing the ties that connected France to other overseas territories, such as Tunisia and Morocco, first granting them autonomy and then finally impendence in 1956. Even so, the French would hold off on releasing Algeria from the colonial ties that bind, with Mendes insisting that Algeria was "part of France."

Nevertheless, native Algerians felt otherwise, and after over one hundred years of French occupation, they, too, were ready for independence. The Algerians would struggle with the French in armed uprising after armed uprising until they finally shook off the French for good in 1962. In the meantime, the French had given up the ghost in Southeast Asia, handing over the baton to the United States, as a communist insurgency in South Vietnam backed by the North threatened to make all of Vietnam a haven for communism.

Unlike the French, the U.S. had no interest in colonialism, but because the insurgents were communist-based, Washington had deep fears of a communist domino effect spiraling out of control in the region. As such, U.S. officials did everything they could to support non-communist South Vietnam. They placed money and later personnel in the region to bolster its defenses against the communist north.

As early as 1954, the U.S. began sending over military advisors. It was not until 1965 that American forces committed themselves entirely to the conflict, a conflict they would ultimately lose in 1975. By this time, the French had washed their hands of Vietnam entirely. France would undergo a mini-Renaissance under that stalwart hero of the Second World War Charles De Gaulle, who came to power in France in 1958.

Mr. De Gaulle would work to forge a closer alliance with other European countries and bolster the French military, a program that included the establishment of a French nuclear arsenal, the latter of which was indeed very important to De Gaulle, who viewed it necessary to break up the virtual monopoly that the U.S. and the then Soviet Union had on nuclear weapons at this time. Even while asserting its independence as a newfound nuclear power, France also sought to strengthen its ties with its European neighbors.

This was especially true as it pertained to what was then known as "West Germany." Yes, even though the Germans had been the arch nemesis that had occupied and so horribly destabilized France, after the war, the rump state of West Germany would become the best friend of postwar France. Having half of their country sliced off and divided by a Berlin Wall, the Germans had their own problems, and the notion of solidarity with its European neighbors had become urgent.

As such, they eagerly signed a "friendship treaty" with France in 1963. But as much as De Gaulle courted closeness with Western European nations, he also courted controversy with the rest of the world. He alienated the United States with both statements and actions that seemed to indicate his desire to drift away from the lockstep that many other Western European states had with the U.S. during the Cold War.

De Gaulle's sudden denunciations of the Vietnam War were most infuriating from an American standpoint. Even though the Americans had essentially inherited the conflict from the French, De Gaulle made headlines in 1966 when he went on the record rejecting U.S. involvement in what he asserted was an "unjust war."

The following year, he managed to even infuriate Canadians when he visited Quebec in 1967 and made statements seeming to encourage French-speaking Quebec to assert its independence from the rest of Canada! And that was not the end of De Gaulle's international exclamation points. That same year, he also managed to enrage Israel and many of Israel's allies when he issued an arms embargo during the Six Day War.

Nevertheless, as much as De Gaulle wished to create a third option between siding with the United States on every issue or having to bow down to Soviet aggression, the genuine threats of the latter would soon make many of De Gaulle's positions seem ridiculous. The danger of Soviet aggression became all too real in 1968 when a demonstration in Czechoslovakia led to a vicious Soviet crackdown that included tanks rolling into Prague.

With the Soviets on the march, De Gaulle's drift away from U.S. foreign policy, which many viewed as being in the best interest of all Western nations, seemed tantamount to suicide at this point. Charles De Gaulle feeling the pressure of his own failed ambition, ultimately resigned from office in 1969. France had found itself adrift in new and uncharted territory and was looking for a friendly place to set anchor.

Chapter 10: France's Evolving Mission in a Globalized World

In its post-war years, France was finding itself as part of an increasingly interconnected and globalized world. Its colonial holdings might have been shed, but even without far-flung colonies, France was able to take full advantage of an increasingly internationalized marketplace that provided France access to an increasing area of goods and services.

But despite the more or less solid economic footing that France found itself on. The political footing was far from certain. Charles De Gaulle had ridden a wave of popularity in the 1960s only to resign in 1969. His resignation prompted a new election and a search for viable candidates. It was ultimately his own prime minister Georges Pompidou who became his successor. Although Pompidou was considered a "Gaullist," even though he was not Gaulle, many believed him to back similar policies and agendas.

But Pompidou proved to be much lower-key than his bombastic predecessor. He refrained from making incendiary remarks in public, and unlike De Gaulle, he expressed much more solidarity with France's traditional allies of Britain and the United States. Pompidou also followed a more traditional "laissez-faire" styled economy, allowing the market to work itself out of its own accord.

And by the 1970s, France was indeed experiencing an economic boom with robust international trade. As was demonstrated by the fact that the average French citizen now had their own cars, washing machines, refrigerators, and televisions. This is in stark contrast to the deprivation experienced in previous years. But perhaps most telling was the rush to equip French homes with phones.

Before Pompidou, only 14 percent of French homes had a working telephone. By the 1980s, however, it is said that that number had risen to 75 percent. It might seem a bit shocking to us today to think that France had been lagging behind the world in these commodities, but the gains made under Pompidou do give us a window into the lack that he encountered upon entering office.

Pompidou's exit was yet another sudden departure in French politics; he died in office on April 2, 1974. As many gains as his administration had made, he had left with a looming economic crisis due to the rising cost of oil. France was very much dependent on oil from the Mideast during this period, and an embargo put in place by oil-producing countries in 1973 led to severe inflation in 1974.

After Pompidou's demise, it was liberal leader Valery Giscard d'Estaing who would take on this economic crisis. Giscard did his best to stem the tide, but the problems seemed almost insurmountable. In the meantime, France would be rocked by yet another oil-fueled economic meltdown in 1979, in the wake of the Iranian Revolution. The west friendly Shah of Iran had been deposed and replaced with an Islamic regime.

Such things did not bode well for the upcoming election held in 1981. Here, the faltering Giscard faced off against the socialist stalwart Francois Mitterrand. Mitterrand was able to capitalize on the economic crisis and other turbulence that had erupted during the Giscard years and ran on a campaign of "*la force tranquille*," or "the tranquil force."

He presented himself as a calm, steady force that would be able to right the floundering French ship. Mitterrand's presentation was convincing enough, and he ultimately managed to squeak out a victory of 51.75 percent to Giscard's 48.24 percent. Now the 1980s belonged to the left wing of French politics. The question was, what would they do with it? The economy was still front and center, but Mitterrand also had some social objectives he wished to achieve.

His first major act while in office was to get rid of France's death penalty, which was officially eliminated from the French legal books in 1981. For a country known for the guillotine, the idea that no one in France, for political reasons or otherwise, would ever have to lose their head again was revolutionary in itself. As it pertains to the economy, the following year, in 1982, Mitterrand embarked upon an approach that probably did more for French finances than anything else during his tenure.

That year, he enabled local representatives at the municipal level to have much more robust control over the spending that went on in their districts. This helped create more oversight and was constructive in the fight against corruption. But it was perhaps Mitterrand's own socialist ambition that did in his administration. After he raised minimum wage, added in extra housing subsidies, medical benefits, and enhanced old age pensions, inflation began to go through the roof.

All of these social programs do not pay for themselves, of course. In a bid to offset their cost, Mitterrand had attempted to tax the wealthiest in France. Yes, in a classic imitation of Robin Hood, this socialist stalwart wished to rob the rich and give to the poor. But his efforts only added to France's already dire state of inflation.

It also did not help that Germany, the United Kingdom, and the United States were going in the opposite direction, enacting deflationary policies by raising interest rates. Soon France's inflationary spending was so out of control and its international interest rates so worthless that the franc itself became just about worthless, as the currency of France became repeatedly devalued.

Stats for economic growth in France from 1981 to 1984 show a growth rate of just 1.5 percent. Socialist or no socialist, Mitterrand was smart enough to know that his policies were not working, and by 1983, he was beginning to sing a different tune. At this point, his administration changed course and began to implement the same deflationary policies being executed by Western Europe and the United States.

On the international stage, the new realities of globalism and increased immigration to France from many of its former colonies were sparking anxieties in mainland France. These anxieties helped fuel the rise of right-wing nationalist, Jean-Marie Le Pen, and his party, the National Front. In light of the growing fear and discontent of the French electorate, the National Front began to gain traction.

At the same time, Mitterrand and his party did not seek to stoke fear and division but to kindle hope and solidarity among all French-speaking peoples across the globe. Starting in 1982, Mitterrand spearheaded international summits dedicated to the "Francophone nations," in which he spoke of his desire for universal understanding between these "carriers of [French] culture."

These efforts appealed to many in both French Canadian and African lands, where France was the dominant language. Mitterrand went into the 1988 elections with much uncertainty but managed to squeak out a win against his opponent Jacques Chirac. Mitterrand, in the meantime, was dealing with a faltering legacy. By the early 1990s, he was seeking anything upon which he could hang his political hat.

With this in mind, Mitterrand introduced proposals in 1992 for the French electorate to vote on the Maastricht Treaty, which was another significant step in European unification since it would help forge a universal European market. The measure passed but barely, with 59 percent voting for it and 49 percent voting against it.

The following year, however, the French economy took another hit when in 1993, French GDP declined, and unemployment skyrocketed. During the parliamentary elections of that same year, Jacque Chirac's party won seats in a landslide victory. This paved the way for Chirac's own election in 1995. Under the Chirac administration, economic conditions began to improve.

In 1998, for example, instead of contracting, the French economy is said to have hit a growth spurt, growing as much as 3.2 percent that year! France was doing well enough that the following year, it felt fully confident to lend its hand in the NATO conflict that had erupted over the former Yugoslavian country Kosovo.

After the eruption of the conflict in the spring of 1999, it is said that France supplied more aircraft fighter jets than any other European nation involved. Later that year, France also played a pivotal part in another step toward European unity by supporting the creation of the "Eurozone" in 1999. France faced an economic downturn in the early 2000s; however, it went bust after the dot-com boom.

The situation was so bad that taxi drivers went on strike in the cities, and farmers used their tractors to block off access to oil refineries. Going into the 2002 election, the situation looked grim, yet Jacques Chirac stunned the world by coming out on top with a landslide win of 82 percent of the vote. The explanation for this feat was simply that there were no other candidates that were at all palatable to the French electorate.

Chirac's main competitor was socialist politician Lionel Jospin and far-right hopeful Jean Marie Le Pen. No one was thrilled with Jospin, and no one was willing to vote a far-right candidate like Le Pen into office. This does much to explain Chirac's landslide win. Even so, the fact that a character like Le Pen picked up as much of the vote as he did prompted the satirical French TV show "Les Guignols d l'Info" to do a skit with a La Pen puppet quietly standing around in the background.

The Le Pen puppet was asked what it was up to, only for it to answer, "Nothing—just waiting." As if all the far right had to do was wait for the French to lose faith in France's more traditional political parties, and the door to the presidency would be opened for them.

Shortly after the election, when the U.S. launched its ill-fated 2003 invasion of Iraq, Chirac inflamed tensions with the U.S. by refusing to participate. Although U.S. President George W. Bush had traveled the world making the case that Iraq had weapons of mass destruction and was connected to terrorist groups, Chirac saw neither the connection nor the necessity of the invasion.

As history would later attest, Chirac seems to have made a wise choice. Iraq was found not to have the weapons of mass destruction that the Bush administration had suggested. And any active connection to terror groups was never adequately proven. Even so, the fact that France snubbed the United States' war efforts would put a dent in U.S./French relations.

In 2007, Chirac was succeeded by his former Prime Minister Nicolas Sarkozy. Although France had sat out the 2003 invasion of Iraq, it did recognize the need to beef up its military. And in 2008, one of the first initiatives Sarkozy embarked upon was modernizing the French army. This meant heavy investment in modern drones, satellites, the latest jet fighters, and even the construction of new nuclear submarines.

Interestingly, even though the French military stayed its hand during the Iraq war, in 2011, during the so-called "Arab Spring" that rocked North Africa, when rebels toppled Kaddafi in Libya, Sarkozy sent in some of those aforementioned fighter jets to lend his support. The reasons for doing this could be argued to be just as questionable as the reasoning behind the invasion of Iraq, but in this instance, Sarkozy decided not to be shy with the use of the French armed forces.

Sarkozy would not win reelection; however, he ultimately lost the presidency to Francois Hollande in 2012. Hollande would, in turn, be succeeded by French President Emanuel Macron in 2017. Macron was then reelected in a nail-biter of an election in 2022. He was running against the older La-Pen's daughter Marine Le Pen. Macron was the first incumbent French president to win reelection since the days of Jacques Chirac back in 2002.

Conclusion: Rising to the Challenge

France is one of the planet's oldest, continuous hubs of human habitation. We must say "human habitation" because although the name "France" has not always been applied to this region, human dwellers have been on the land for many millions of years. As those who inhabited this land first began to show up in the annals of recorded history, they were known as Gauls, and France itself became the land of Gaul as far as the Romans were concerned.

After the fall of the Roman Empire from which ancient France had been incorporated, a tribe known as the "Franks" came to prominence, and it was from them that the name "France" was ultimately derived. Under the Franks, we first saw the Merovingian, the Carolingian, and finally, the Capet dynasties that would bring a long line of French kings to the throne.

This procession of royal administrations would be interrupted by the French Revolution, which would rock not just France but also society in general to its very core. The French Revolution would bring forth tremendous bloodshed, as kings, queens, and the average citizen alike were all trampled under the wheels of revolutionary fervor.

But even so, the French Revolution, despite the violence that it brought about, also enshrined some of the most enduring aspects of modern law, such as a free press and individual rights that today many in the Western world take for granted. Even so, the drafters of these laws would not always enjoy them. The Revolution would ultimately devolve into a dictatorship under Napoleon Bonaparte, and Bonaparte would lead much of the world into battle against him.

After the Napoleonic wars finally came to a close, with Napoleon's final abdication in 1815, France would temporarily go back to the Bourbon monarchy. However, this was just a brief interlude before Napoleon III would rise to the throne in the aftermath of the wave of revolutions in 1848. Napoleon III sought to rebuild his uncle's empire, and in many ways, he was successful. It was under Napoleon III that France would regain much of its lost prestige through military successes and the acquisition of territory all over the globe.

Napoleon III would be toppled in 1870 by rising German power in the form of Prussia. The toppling of the French would have significant ramifications in the form of the unification of Italy and Germany. France's days of Empire in Europe seemed to be over, but its colonial empire remained. This it would not lose until World War Two forced much of France's overseas holdings out of its hands.

In the aftermath of World War Two, France tried its best to recoup and regain some of its lost overseas territory, especially Vietnam and Algeria, but ultimately had to wash its hands of them. With the loss of its past imperial possessions, France began to turn inward and ultimately began to look toward the European neighborhood for the future.

It was around this time, of course, that the first steps toward the European Union began. France was always at the forefront of this charge, first with the establishment of the European Commission and then the creation of the Eurozone; all of these things helped to forge what we now call the EU.

France continues to lead the way no matter what factors are in play or the situation. France has always played a unique role in the region, and its mission continues to evolve. That said, France faced significant turbulence in the late 2010s, with an upsurge of terror attacks aimed at destabilizing French society.

First, there was the Charlie Hebdo attack in January 2015, only to suffer through the November terror attacks that were staged in Paris, killing over one hundred people. There was also a truck bomb attack in Nice, France, in 2016, just prior to Emanuel Macron's rise to power in 2017. These are some pretty fierce headwinds for anyone to deal with.

Even so, judging from France's long history, the land of the Franks will undoubtedly rise to the challenge.

Here's another book by Enthralling History that you might like

Free limited time bonus

Stop for a moment. We have a free bonus set up for you. The problem is this: we forget 90% of everything that we read after 7 days. Crazy fact, right? Here's the solution: we've created a printable, 1-page pdf summary for this book that you're reading now. All you have to do to get your free pdf summary is to go to the following website:

https://livetolearn.lpages.co/enthrallinghistory/

Once you do, it will be intuitive. Enjoy, and thank you!

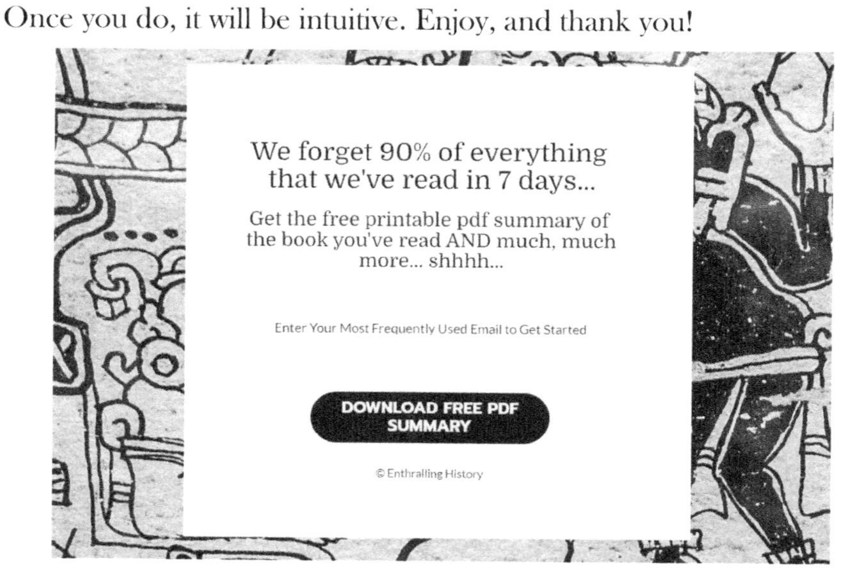

Appendix A: Further Reading and References

Alexander, Martin S. *French History Since Napoleon*. 1999.
Haine, W. Scott. *The History of France*. 2000.
Popkin, Jeremy D. *A History of Modern France*. 1994.
Price, Roger. *A Concise History of France*. 2005.